Peace and the War Industry

Second Edition

Edited by
KENNETH E. BOULDING

Transaction Books
New Brunswick, New Jersey
Distributed by E.P. Dutton & Co., Inc.

Transaction Books
Rutgers University
New Brunswick, New Jersey 08903

Library of Congress Catalog Card Number: 72-87664
ISBN: 0-87855-052-6 (cloth); 0-87855-545-5 (paper)

Printed in the United States of America

Peace and the War Industry

transaction/**Society** Book Series

Contents

Preface

For the past decade, *trans*action, and now **Society**, has dedicated itself to the task of reporting the strains and conflicts within the American system. But the magazine has done more than this. It has pioneered in social programs for changing the social order, offered the kind of analysis that has permanently restructured the terms of the "dialogue" between peoples and publics, and offered the sort of prognosis that makes for real alterations in economic and political policies directly affecting our lives.

The work done in the magazine has crossed disciplinary boundaries. This represents much more than simple cross-disciplinary "team efforts." It embodies rather a recognition that the social world cannot be easily carved into neat academic disciplines; that, indeed, the study of the experience of blacks in American ghettos, or the manifold uses and abuses of agencies of law enforcement, or the sorts of overseas policies that lead to the celebration of some dictatorships and the condemnation of others, can best be examined from many viewpoints and from the vantage points of many disciplines.

The editors of **Society** magazine are now making available in permanent form the most important work done in the magazine, supplemented in some cases by additional materials edited to reflect the tone and style developed over the years by *trans*action. Like the magazine, this series of books demonstrates the superiority of starting with real world problems and searching out practical solutions, over the zealous guardianship of professional boundaries. Indeed, it is precisely this approach that has elicited enthusiastic support from leading American social scientists, many of whom are represented among the editors of these volumes.

The subject matter of these books concerns social changes and social policies that have aroused the long-standing needs and present-day anxieties of us all. These changes are in organizational lifestyles, concepts of human ability and intelligence, changing patterns of norms and morals, the relationship of social conditions to physical and biological environments, and in the status of social science with respect to national policy making. The editors feel that many of these articles have withstood the test of time, and match in durable interest the best of available social science literature. This collection of essays, then, attempts to address itself to immediate issues without violating the basic insights derived from the classical literature in the various fields of social science.

As the political crises of the sixties have given way to the economic crunch of the seventies, the social scientists involved as editors and authors of this series have gone beyond observation of critical areas, and have entered into the vital and difficult tasks of explanation and interpretation. They have defined issues in a way that makes solutions possible. They have provided answers as well as asked the right questions. These books, based as they are upon the best materials from *tran*saction/**Society** magazine, are dedicated to highlighting social problems alone, and beyond that, to establishing guidelines for social solutions based on the social sciences.

The remarkable success of the book series to date is indicative of the need for such "fastbacks" in college course work and, no less, in the everyday needs of busy people who have not surrendered the need to know, nor the lively sense required to satisfy such knowledge needs. It is also plain that what superficially appeared as a random selection of articles on the basis of subject alone, in fact, represented a careful concern for materials that are addressed to issues at the shank and marrow of society. It is the distillation of the best of these, systematically arranged, that appears in these volumes.

THE EDITORS
*tran*saction/**Society**

The Deadly Industry:
War and the International System

KENNETH E. BOULDING

We have now had reasonably accurate national accounts for the United States for over 40 years; that is, for the effective lifetimes of those who are now getting into powerful, decision-making positions. The importance of this cumulative record is hard to overestimate. It does for economics what the painstaking collection of long-time observation of the movements of the planets did for astronomy: it gives us a framework within which everything can be seen in proportion. One suspects that most errors in judgment and decision arise because the world is perceived in terms of what is salient rather than what is significant or in high proportion. The collection of records of this kind, however, enables us to see what the proportions actually are.

In dealing with the proportions of the economy, the first question one must ask is: What is the total, what is 100 percent? The gross national product is often taken

1

as the measure of the total size of the economy. This, how-ever, is unsatisfactory, especially in a period of unemploy-ment, because it does not measure the capacity of the sys-tem, but only what is realized. It is necessary, therefore, to develop a concept of a "gross capacity product," which represents what the gross product would have been if there had been no unemployment. This calculation is not easy. As a very rough measure we could take the gross national product and increase it by the proportion of the labor force unemployed. The gross capacity product then would be defined by the following formula:

$$\text{Gross capacity product} = \text{gross national product} \times \frac{100}{100 - e}$$

where e is the proportion of the labor force unemployed. This measure is subject to two errors which operate in opposite directions and hopefully may be subject to the law of benevolently countervailing error. The first is that the unemployed would presumably be less productive than the employed labor force if they were actually employed, so that the above measure exaggerates the gross capacity product by an amount which depends on how low the pro-ductivity of the unemployed actually is. On the other hand, the official unemployment figure underestimates un-employment because it does not take account of under-employment, part-time work and so on. The gross national product also underestimates the contribution of housewives and nonmarketable labor. These two factors would make our measure of the gross capacity product too small. One may hope, though, that these two errors in opposite di-rections will cancel each other out, and our measure may be taken as at least a simple index which may not be wholly accurate in the more extreme years.

Figure 1, then, shows the history of the last 43 years in terms of the proportionate structure of the gross capacity product. We see the depth of the Great Depression in the unrealized product—almost 25 percent in 1933. We see also that the New Deal was a failure in terms of its major objective to solve the unemployment problem, even though it had some important long-run spin-offs, in terms of social security and the like. The recovery from the bottom of 1933 was very slow. Even in 1937 the unrealized product was still 15 percent, and the depression of 1938 pushed us back almost to the position at the beginning of 1932; even by 1940 we had only gotten back to the position of 1936. The losses here are enormous and represent something like two whole years' product in the 12 years from 1929 to 1941.

We see the Second World War vividly as an enormous expansion of national defense, from under 1 percent of the gross capacity product during the depression to over 40 percent in 1942, 1943 and 1944. We see very vividly the source of what I have sometimes called the "great American myth"—that only a large war industry can save us from depression, for in the memory of those who lived through this period, this was, in fact, their experience. The war did reduce unemployment to virtually zero, and it was paid for half out of the unemployment that might have been there otherwise and about half by reduction in the other elements of the system, especially civilian government, gross private domestic investment and personal consumption.

We next see the Great Disarmament of 1945 and 1946. It is odd that this has left so little impression on the American consciousness. It was achieved with unemployment never rising above 3 percent and with astonishingly little dislocation. Its history has never been properly written, but it is one of the most extraordinary episodes in all of economic history. Here almost a third of the economic

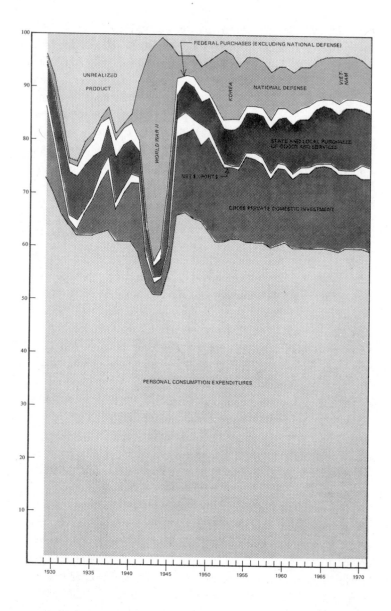

activity of a large and very complex society was transferred from the war industry into civilian purposes. It was accomplished in little over a year and with an incredibly small amount of disruption.

We then see the first Cold War rearmament from 1950 into the Korean War, which reached its maximum in 1953, but continued through the fifties into the sixties, with national defense occupying from 8 to 10 percent of the gross capacity product. This is a very marked structural change from the thirties and is perhaps among the three major structural changes in the American economy in this period, the other two being the decline of agriculture and the decline of the whole private sector of the economy, especially personal consumption expenditure, in the face of expanding government. We should note, however, the period from 1963 to 1965, when national defense as a proportion of gross capacity product declined and unemployment likewise declined. From 1965 to 1968 we see the expansion due to the Vietnam War, which from the American point of view is almost frighteningly small.

An extraordinarily interesting feature of the last 20 years has been the stability in the proportionate structure in the American economy in many ways. Personal consumption structure was squeezed by the expansion of the military, but has remained virtually stable as a proportion of the gross capacity product, at close to 60 percent ever since 1951. Gross private domestic investment, likewise, has been extraordinarily stable, apart from a small cyclical fluctuation, a good part of which is in inventory. The total government sector is, likewise, astonishingly stable, and one of the striking features of the sixties is the way in which the civilian government proportion of the economy (state, local and federal) rose in response to the declining proportion of national defense. It must be remembered at all times that these are proportionate, not absolute, figures, and that in this period, of course, the gross capacity product itself rose, in fact more than doubled in real terms. The contrast between the period of great instability in the proportionate structure before, say, 1946 and the period of relative stability since, is almost certainly beginning to have an effect on our national attitudes and our perception of the world.

Paradoxically enough, one of the principal consequences of full employment is the reappearance of scarcity. The critical question here is: What goes down when national defense expenditure goes up by a dollar? If what goes down is simply unemployment, as in the "great American myth," then national defense is virtually costless in real terms. If, however, we have approximately full employment, or at least moderately full employment, as we have had for the last 20 years, scarcity suddenly reasserts itself, and it becomes very clear that a dollar added to the military is a dollar taken away from somebody else, and then the question becomes of great importance: Who is the somebody else? Unfortunately, this is a question that is by no means easy to answer, for components of the economy may go up and down for a great variety of reasons. We cannot simply assume that if something goes down when the military goes up that this was a cause-and-effect relationship. If, for instance, we look at the components of personal consumption expenditure, we find that food and clothing have gone down quite sharply as a proportion of the gross capacity product, but this is because we are getting richer, according to the well-known "Engle's Law" in economics (the singular Engle, not the plural Engles). If we were to bring the war industry down to the proportionate level of the thirties, assuming that we maintained full employment (with modern techniques it is fairly easy to make this calculation), it is not altogether easy to say what factor would expand. The evidence suggests that personal consumption would expand, as would civilian government, but in what proportions it is not easy to say, and indeed this may well depend on the particular policies and sentiments which happen to be in operation at the time. If we are in a Galbraithian mood, as we seem to have been in the last ten years or so, with the remarkable expansion of civilian government, we may expect this expansion to continue. On the other hand, if we are in a more private mood, we are well aware that the biggest bite out of the economy which the war industry imposes is the bite out of personal consumption expenditure, which is now only 60 percent of the gross capacity product, as against 72 percent in 1929. In such a case, the pressure may be for tax reduction and even budget deficits which will expand the private sector and the personal sector.

There are some interesting, but equally unanswerable, political questions involved in this rather sketchy economic analysis. The important question here in the face of an increasing consciousness of scarcity is what kind of political coalitions are likely to form against the war industry. Coalitions tend to form among people who have a common sense that their particular ox is being gored, even though they may have very different oxen. The political coalition that is most likely to form against the war industry would seem to be, from this analysis, a rather odd combination of Left and Right, the people who feel that the war industry is biting into civilian government and especially, what is not shown in the figure, into government transfers, that is, grants and redistributions and on the other hand, the people, who feel that the real bite is out of the private household sector. The combination of little old ladies in tennis shoes and bright-eyed left-wing bureaucrats may sound too implausible even to mention, but stranger things have happened, and this would seem to be where the combination of economic interests lies.

Behind all this argument lies an assumption that the national defense component is politically flexible in response to domestic demands. Economists, on the whole, have regarded national defense as essentially exogenous (that is, determined by forces completely outside the economic system and especially the domestic economic system). This is the myth of military necessity, which the military, of course, is not slow to foster. In fact, however, it is a myth. The Congressional votes for appropriations for national defense, which essentially determine the size of the war industry, depend on a great variety of circumstances, and especially on the current concept of the national image and the national interest. One of the important things that seems to be happening at the moment is the realization that the national interest is a variable, not a constant of the system, and that it is, in fact, simply what the nation is interested in. All organizations, and the nation is no exception, are interested in survival, but the nation is interested in many other things beside this, and if national defense were directed solely at survival it would almost certainly cost much less than it does now and would comprise a very different set of resources.

The rise in the proportion of the gross capacity product occupied by the war industry is partly a reflection of a real change in the international system itself which has brought us all so uncomfortably close together, but it is also a reflection in the change in the national image, from a nation lying somewhat on the periphery of the international system (which was the way we visualized ourselves even up to the Second World War), to a nation which is central in the international system. This is what I have sometimes called the "mantle of Elijah complex," the image being that the mantle of the British Empire has fallen on us. This particularly seems to have been the case with the Democrats. Both Acheson and Rusk had a strong sense of having been covered with the mantle of Elijah, which came fluttering down from the British as they proceeded to descend from the cloudy heights of great power status and built themselves a comfortable little welfare state on terra firma. The British abandonment of the image of being a great power was partly a result of the rising costs of being a power, but also a result of the increasing domestic pressures, especially on the government sector. We have seen something of the same thing happening in this country in the last 15 years, at least in the slow encroachment of civilian government on national defense, which was particularly noticeable until 1965. The criticism of the Vietnam War, which is surely the most unpopular war in American history, has been a result not only of its uselessness in terms of any conceivable national interest, but also, I think, because of the reawakened sense of "scarcity" and the feeling that the Vietnam War was pressing on much more urgent domestic priorities, especially in the government sector.

In conclusion, then, the international system can be thought of as a particular segment of the total world social system. The war industry, which may be defined as that part of the economic output purchased by military budgets, comprises a very large part of the international system. In terms of the world economy, the world war industry is of the order of 5 to 10 percent of the world product. The international system outside the war industry —the state departments, foreign offices, diplomats and so on—occupies a very tiny fraction of the total economy. The international system occupies a larger proportion of the communications system, such as history books and newspapers. It has a saliency that makes its quantitative impact on the totality of human life hard to measure. For example, it is doubtful that more than 10 percent of the total output of communications deals with the international system in terms of sheer quantity, but it seems to loom larger than that, perhaps because it is subject to sudden ups and downs and it is also perceived as very dangerous.

In the United States the war industry has varied from 0.6 percent of the gross national product to about 42 percent over the last 40 years, and is now running at about 6.8 percent, of which about 2 to 3 percent involves the Vietnam War. The war industry is a much larger part of the political system than it is of the economic system. Thus, in the United States the war industry occupies some 30.6 percent of the total government sector of the economy, including federal, state and local. The international system must take a large proportion of the time of the President, although a much smaller proportion of the time of Congress.

There is a widespread feeling, which most of the papers in this collection reflect, that the international system is dangerous and expensive, that its legitimacy has been declining and that an ardent search for a better solution to this problem is very much in order. The scientific revolution has made an enormous impact on the international system and has, I believe, made it obsolete. The international system is the major part of that segment of the total social system where threat predominates as a social organizer. In internal political systems, we have what might be called a legitimated threat-submission system, in which people pay their taxes and submit to laws, partly because they approve of doing so in principle, and partly because, if they don't, they will get into trouble. The international system is characterized primarily by deterrence (that is, a threat-counterthreat system): "If you do something nasty to me, I will do something nasty to you." The principal product of the war industry is threat capability, that is, the capability of carrying out threats by being able to produce negative commodities or "bads." The threat system has a much lower horizon of development than the exchange system, in which we persuade others to do something for us by offering them goods rather than threatening to give them "bads." The main difficulty with the threat system is that it is most effective when the threats are not carried out (that is, when they are credible enough to influence behavior), but unless they are occasionally carried out they cease to be credible. The carrying out of a threat, though, is often more costly to the threatener than it is to the victim. This makes the whole economics of the threat system very peculiar.

One of the real problems of the international system has been the absence of adequate theory. We have had a pretty good theory of the exchange system for a long time now. This is economics. The theory of the threat system, and especially the theory of the interaction between the threat system and the exchange system, is still in a rather primitive stage.

I am not suggesting, of course, that these economic considerations are a sufficient, or even a prime, explanation of the sort of things that are going on and which are reflected in the articles in this volume. The international system itself is primarily a political system in the sense that it is based much more on threat than on exchange. The interrelations between the exchange system and the threat system, however, have suddenly become of great interest and, one suspects, of much greater importance than they have been in the past, though there are theoretical problems here that we are still very far from having solved. These one can recommend with great enthusiasm to the social scientists whose work in this area will undoubtedly continue to be published in *trans*action/*Society*.

Another area of research which is reflected in several papers in this volume might be called the "cultural anthropology" of the relevant subcultures within the international system, particularly, of course, the subculture of the military and its interface with civilian government. These cultures tend to get isolated from the rest of society. This is perhaps particularly true of the military culture, which in almost every society is a "ghetto," divided from the rest of society by the sharp wall of our ambivalence toward it. It is not surprising that it produces ingrown pathological models of behavior and images of the world, which can have disastrous effects on the society which it is supposed to defend. There is a good deal of evidence for the proposition that a nation's own war industry is apt to do more damage to it, economically, politically and spiritually, than any enemy war industry. Yet people submit to these injuries because they diminish the subjective uncertainty of the damage which external forces might do to an undefended nation. One of the greatest needs of the social sciences is a clearer understanding of the dynamics of cultural pathology—that is, how things go from bad to worse. There are all too many examples of these processes in this volume. The international system has an almost indubitable right to the doubtful title "the most pathological subsystem within the whole sphere of human society." It now costs over $200 billion a year, and what we seem to be buying with this is a positive probability of almost irretrievable disaster.

One of the hopeful things, oddly enough, in the present situation, is that the cultures of the international system are on the whole highly hierarchical. The armed forces, the executive branch of government and the Catholic Church are perhaps the three most hierarchical cultures of the world. Hierarchical cultures, however, are highly vulnerable to change at the top. A small stone set rolling at the top of a hierarchy can create an avalanche lower down. The impact of Pope John XXII on the Catholic Church and of President Nixon, especially in his visit to China, and the Soviet Union on American foreign policy, may be quite comparable. Social scientists, who have written most of the essays of this volume, and to whom this volume on the whole is addressed, should certainly not cultivate delusions of grandeur. Nevertheless they do contribute to a change in climate, and a change in climate may set off the avalanches of hierarchy. We may even have to concern ourselves with building a few defensive walls so that the avalanches will do more good than harm.

The selections in this volume are topical and they represent applied social science rather than basic theory, though some of them represent rigorous empirical work. Some readers, indeed, may regard them as merely straws in the wind. Nevertheless, it is a big wind that is blowing, and it suggests that a radical transformation in our whole set of perceptions about the international system may not be far away. Because of their topical nature they have been arranged in chronological order, dating from 1964 to 1972. Anyone who wants to know what has been going on in these years at the frontiers of thought and research about the international system, somewhat removed from the established citadels of the conventional wisdom, will find these essays most rewarding.

University of Colorado
Boulder, Colorado

Paradoxes of the Warfare State

ELWIN H. POWELL

Today the preparation for war is the central activity of the modern nation. The world "spends" over $100 billion a year on war, half coming from the United States, a fourth from the Soviet Union, with the remainder shared by other major powers. In the United States the annual expenditures for defense procurement alone are, according to a U. S. Congressional committee, "twice as large as the total net farm income of the nation ... almost twice as large as the total U. S. expenditure for public education." The 1964 defense budget of 56 billion will consume 65 percent of the tax dollar, provide employment for over 10 percent of the labor force and generate some $110 billion in economic activity.

When then are the social consequences of this massive "war" effort? In the early 1950's Harold Lasswell could foresee a "thickening atmosphere of suspicion" as the superstates each became monolithic and as the democratic process died " by slow strangulation." Yet insofar as the war operation has involved a real conflict, not merely an imposture, it has brought certain beneficial changes in "world society." The Soviet need to prosecute the "cold war" is dissolving its own "iron curtain" just as the American response to the Soviet challenge has broken down our tradition and practice of isolationism. Contrary to George Orwell's anticipation, the two systems have not remained "inviolate within their own boundaries." And conflict, as Lewis Coser has pointed out "establishes relations where none may have existed before."

When neither side can annihilate the other and still continue to function as a unit, then conflict is often transmuted into accommodation, and in time accommodation becomes cooperation. Faint hints of the subsiding of world tension are even now apparent and could bring about a wilting of the superstates; indeed, signs of the breakup of war-created alliances of both East and West are already discernible.

The warfare state calls into being its own antithesis, perhaps leading eventually to a new synthesis which none of us can now foresee. The growth of the military-industrial complex has generated counter-currents which seem to contradict the very premises of the garrison state. These unintended consequences of war preparation can be viewed as a series of interrelated paradoxes.

Paradox I: The military-industrial complex does not engender militarism: "Militarism is not so much the propensity to wage war," writes Hans Speier, "as the organization of the civilian sector after the model of the military establishment. A society is militaristic if its civilian members behave like soldiers, value discipline above freedom, pay more respect to valor than to work."

Distinctions between military and civilian life are being obliterated: The United States military establishment is modeled after the business corporation, and not conversely; generals behave like board chairmen, soldiers like clerks. As Morris Janowitz notes, within the military there has been a "shift or organizational authority from discipline based on domination, to organization control involving manipulation." The danger of war today grows out of the finely honed rationality of gamesmanship; it does not stem from what Bertrand Russell calls "the ferocious ... prejudices ... of the military-industrial fanatics."

Professional soldiers are seldom militant. The first requirement of military life is not belligerence but obedience. For an army to become a useful instrument of policy it must be stripped of fanaticism. As Hoffman Nickerson writes: "Professional soldiers are craftsmen ... you do not have to excite them by telling them their enemies are fiends." In the Thurmond hearings on troop indoctrination, General Shoup of the Marine Corps said that he did not want his men to "hate the enemy" because hate engendered (and depended upon) fear, which breeds defeatism and reduces fighting efficiency.

It is primarily in unstable societies that officer corps are insurrectionary; normally the military is content to follow and obey. In the United States, military presidents from Grant to Eisenhower have been mild and passive; they are usually less bellicose than our idealists. The General Walkers are atypical. Military men in foreign-policy positions have proved no more aggressive than civilians; in fact, says Walter Millis, they have often had to "hold back the sporadic and truculent impulses of political people and diplomats ..." The training of the professional soldier and the codes of military life create a rather cautious outlook.

But what of the industrialist? An erratic ferocity was

perhaps the dominant trait of early capitalism, of the Robber Barons. However, corporate capitalism today calls forth a different style of leadership—contrast McNamara with Henry Ford I. The managerial elite is now rarely fanatical and the psychopathic types are usually eliminated in the long climb up the organization pyramid. "The corporate manager today," writes A. A. Berle, "is essentially a civil servant ... There is common interest among corporation administrators in maintaining conditions permitting them to act with a minimum of control, and their enterprises to go on working; and there is a common desire for an orderly system in which they play a prominent part."

Monopoly has curtailed risk in capitalist enterprise and the rationalization of economic life has curbed "adventurism," in both business and politics. Like the medieval church, the primary aim of the modern corporation is continuity. Corporate capitalism engenders a confused conservatism, which if fatuous is not ferocious.

While big business may speak the muted rhetoric of the cold war, it still seems more interested in salesmanship than anticommunism. (The Chamber of Commerce and the head of the New York Stock Exchange backed the recent wheat deal with the Soviet Union and the president of the Chamber has called for trade with Red China.) Most large corporations have not supported the radical right. Fred Cook points out that leading defense contractors (Boeing, Lockheed, General Electric) have used rightist propaganda (Communism on the Map, writings by Fred Schwartz) for public relations purposes, and that an ex-General Motors president made a $300,000 contribution to the anti-communism school of Harding College in Arkansas. But when the big money has to go to

Arkansas to find an ideologist, the danger cannot be quite as grave as Cook suggests. Fifty years ago it could buy spokesmen at Harvard and Yale.

All established corporate structures are conservative, and regard the overly-zealous—the fanatic—as more disruptive than the dissenter. In the Middle Ages the church isolated its religious zealots in monasteries; today the Russian leadership has curtailed its reactionary Stalinists just as the American establishment has sought to control its Birchites. Big business "leans" to the right; big communism "leans" to the left; but probably both would accept a harmonious center position.

Both the Soviet and the American elite have advocated competitive or peaceful coexistence. Erich Fromm contends that while the Soviet elite uses the language of revolution it is, at bottom, concerned with the preservation of the communist establishment. A. A. Berle, the most articulate spokesman of corporate capitalism writes:

> Assuming continued peace, in any long view the American and Soviet systems would seem to be converging rather than diverging so far as their organizational and many of their economic aspects are concerned ... (There is) no essential reason (why they cannot cooperate) provided cooperation is real and not an attempt to weaken the other, awaiting the movement of ultimate conflict.

Paradox II: The pressure for war comes from the public: Mass democracy generates a unique pressure for war: it fosters a climate of irresponsibility while it frustrates the urge for heroic action. The demagogue who cries for war usually finds a following, not because people are bloodthirsty, but because the call for valor and sacrifice elevates them above the dreary routines of peace. People have rather enthusiastically supported every war since the

Napoleonic period and there are many indications that men "enjoy" war; suicide rates decline, birth rates rise. During the war the economy runs in high gear, and confining social patterns are suspended. War is thus a liberating experience to those whose peacetime existence is devoid of excitement and challenge. Consequently, peace movements have never captured the popular imagination.

Immediately before World War I, radicals proclaimed that the conflict would be terminated through a general strike, should the oligarchy be foolish enough to launch a war. But as Norman Thomas once remarked, the war had been in motion scarcely a week before socialists were killing one another just as if they were Christians. In all countries, writes Raymond Aron, "(there was) an explosion of national fervor. Patriotism overrode social resentments and revolutionary aspirations." Since World War I, organized mass opposition to war has all but vanished. The peace issue has almost no appeal to the electorate. In the 1962 Congressional elections, none of the candidates who made peace a principle issue was elected to office, and those who ran as independents received a bare 1 percent of the primary vote.

For most men modern life requires a concentration on immediacies. Reflecting on public indifference to disarmament, Nathan Glazer writes: "People understand the possible dangers of atomic war well enough, but it appears a distant and abstract idea as against the immediate prospect of unemployment, relocation, retraining." The people live from day to day, elected officials from term to term; neither is disposed to take a long view of historical developments nor feels a stake in the remote future.

It might well be argued that the power elite, or the ruling class, has a more clearly defined "rational self-interest" in avoiding war than does the general public. It is not control by the elite but the absence of clear lines of authority which creates the greatest danger of war.

Paradox III: Increased military power reduces military security: In a world which is an amalgam of 1984 and Alice in Wonderland, not the least of the contradictions is the fact that any increase in weaponry reduces the security of everyone. It is disarmament and arms control, therefore, that become a "defense measure." Actually the concept of defense has been outmoded and current strategy is based on deterrence. But as Norman Cousins observes: "one nation's deterrence is another's incentive." The United States atomic monopoly did not prevent but stimulated Russian development of the bomb, and the success of Soviet rocketry was a prime incentive for our own missile program. The mutual possession of nuclear weapons with instant delivery systems, tends to nullify the value of possessing them. As Liddel-Hart writes, "the natural consequence of nuclear parity is nuclear nullity." The thermonuclear stalemate has now been given official recognition by Secretary of Defense McNamara:

> We are approaching an era when it will become increasingly improbable that either side could destroy a sufficiently large portion of the other's strategic force, either by surprise or otherwise, to preclude a devastating retaliatory blow.

With the thermonuclear stalemate and the dawning recognition that the "communist threat" is not primarily military, interest has turned to other forms of war. "The cold war," writes Robert Osgood, "is neither war nor peace in the orthodox sense, but a continuing struggle for power, waged by political, psychological and economic means as well as by a variety of military and semi-military means."

As the focus of conflict shifts from the organized world of nation-states to the grey chaos of colonial countries, conventional as well as nuclear arms are rendered useless. Attention has thus shifted to guerilla war which is a matter of politics, not arms. To succeed, guerilla operations must elicit the support of native populations. Confronted with revolutionary movements, the U. S. military apparatus has repeatedly proved impotent. It could do nothing about the "Cuban problem." And our military aid to South America, says Senator Wayne Morse, "is the most important cause in the deterioration of U.S.-Latin American relations." To this extent the military program has increased, not diminished, our military insecurity.

Strategists need to rethink the concept of "preventive war." Prevention is not preemption but the elimination of the sources of conflict. "Our problem," says George Kennan, "is no longer to prevent people from acquiring the ability to destroy us—it is too late for that. Our problem is to see that they do not have the will or the incentive to do it."

Paradox IV: The military program has undermined the garrison state: The revolution in warfare has destroyed the mass army and with it the psychological foundations of the garrison state. The war emotions of hate of the enemy induce the population to make the sacrifices needed to maintain the war machine. In 1948 the critics of universal military training saw in it the dreaded spectre of goosestepping Nazis. But no one who has actually observed the college R.O.T.C. or the play-warring of the national guard (or regular Army) could see the program as the mother of the garrison state. Military service has been sold to both the public and the participants in terms of rational civilian values—upward mobility, adventure, sociability. There is hardly a mention of honor and patriotism, the values of classic militarism.

Since the time of Caesar the military has been an avenue of social ascent and, to that extent, a democratizing force. Today in America military service is often a way out and up for men from deprived groups—the Southern Negro, the slum boy. The 2.5 million men under arms probably have a more meaningful life than would otherwise be available to them. As civilians they would only swell the ranks of the unemployed by another 30 percent. Ideally, better use could be made of unemployable labor; but given the structure of American society a large army is perhaps the lesser of domestic evils. The results of universal military training have been benign, if not beneficial. Conventional forces today, like Roman legions, are primarily administrative rather than fighting organizations.

In addition the new machinery of war has called into being a class of technicians which bears no resemblance to military men of the past. In psychology and style of life, the military scientist or the engineer working on a missile or space assignment is no different from his colleagues in a university or a corporation. Moreover, the need for skilled specialists now enables the government to define education as a form of defense. Of the $700 million in financial aid directly to college students, $246 million comes from the federal government, and $100 million of that amount as "national defense scholarship loans." Over half of the "research and development" of the country is financed by the federal govenment ($5.6 billion in 1959), five-sixths of it directly through the defense department. But research and development is not inseparably linked to the war effort; it is a way in which the arms race could be formed into a space race without disrupting the economy. The new war technology has made disarmament economically feasible.

Mass war production has passed away with the mass army. Heavy industry areas—such as the Great Lakes region—are even now experiencing the economic impact of disarmament as defense-spending shifts to the east and west coasts. Even with record defense expenditures, un-employment increases and economic stagnation continues throughout much of the country.

When it is no longer possible for Senators and Congress-men to obtain defense contracts for their states, they may begin to look for other forms of government subsidy. "Economics," says Fred Cook, "has begun to throw its powerful arguments behind the idealistic and humanitarian pleas of those who are seeking to stop the arms race." Even so, it is virtually inconceivable that our vast military establishment would ever be dismantled. But it might be possible to turn the powers of the Pentagon to other purposes than destructive warfare.

Paradox V: The pentagon as an instrument of social reconstruction: Inherently our military establishment is neither reactionary nor progressive; it merely carries out the mandate of the state. Historically, armies have served mainly as a police force—from 1890 to 1917 strike-breaking was the main function of the U. S. Army, but in the 1950's the same organization was used to enforce school integra-tion. The U. S. Army has also carried out valuable engineer-ing projects: surveying and exploration in the early 19th century, flood control and dam building in the 1930's. Conceivably the Pentagon could become an institution for social and economic planning. It does have both the "know how" and the power to implement the vast changes which our society requires. There is no intrinsic reason why the power of the Pentagon cannot be used constructively in economic policy, education, urban renewal or even social welfare—both at home and abroad.

Even the military aid program has more constructive potentialities than is often realized. As colonial countries pass from tribal-feudalism to nationalism the native armies are expanded and become "instruments of modernization ... extending literacy and technological and administrative skills ... as well as building certain social overhead capital (sewer and transit systems, surveying, etc.) ... Burma, Turkey and Nasser's Egypt are cases in point." Unfortunately, most U. S. military aid goes to support reactionary and repressive regimes—Korea, Taiwan, and South Vietnam receive over half of all U. S. military aid to underdeveloped countries. But that is the result of a political, not a military decision. That the military can carry out a "democratizing program" was shown by MacArthur in Japan. In fact, the Pentagon could probably handle foreign aid more effectively than civilian agencies, since it has the power to resist local business and feudalistic pressures. For the same reasons it might also be used to cope with certain domestic problems such as urban renewal.

Paradox VI: The war emotions are potentially creative: The warfare state has superseded the welfare state, a generally lamented change. Yet if the basic meaning of war and welfare could be disentangled the former might appear the nobler cause. After 20 centuries of Christianity the concept of welfare still has little force. In western culture welfare comes as an afterthought, to be attended to only when the main business of life is settled. Singularly devoid of idealism and imagination, the welfare state was conceived and executed in the joyless spirit of the dole. Welfare, as understood and practiced in our time, makes the individual a passive recipient. Warfare, on the other hand, transforms the person into an active participant in a collective enterprise and thus evokes the altruism in men. As Gilbert Murray wrote in the aftermath of World War I:

"It is not that men want to kill, but they want to face death and peril. They want to put forth for one great moment the extreme effort of mind and body of which they are capable. They want to do it for others, for some great unspecified cause, so that if they live those whom they saved will adore them, and if they die multitudes will bless their memory."

Human society itself seems to have grown out of a union for common defense. "Only by the imperative need for combination in war" writes Herbert Spencer, "were primitive men led into cooperation." Robert Ardry contends that man himself descended from a now-extinct weapon-using ape. The machinery of war precedes the technology of agriculture and commerce, and all our evolution has not washed out the love of war.

The appeal of war is too profound to be neutralized by the sensible arguments of rational men. As William James noted half a century ago "the horrors make the fascination of war." Men need to prove to themselves and others that they are unafraid; they embrace the horror of war in order to conquer their own fears. When the peace movement points to the suicidal destructiveness of modern war, it provokes others to profess their willingness to die for civilization and thus demonstrate their bravery. "War is the province of danger," writes Clausewitz, "and therefore courage above all things is the first quality of the warrior ... war is the province of physical exertion and suffering ... war is the province of chance." Danger, courage, exertion, suffering, chance—the benefits of peace seem ignoble by comparison. That is why the search for peace will fail if peace is conceived as merely the absence of war.

"War," writes William James, "has been the only force that can discipline (i.e. integrate) a whole community, and until an equivalent discipline is organized, I believe that war must have its way." *The task is not to eliminate war but to change its object;* the task is to wage war against the natural enemies of all mankind, as President Kennedy said in his inaugural address. The "real enemy" is not totalitarian communism but the dehumanization of man which has resulted from the cataclysmic social upheaval of our time.

Can science be conceived as a battle for truth, or education as a war against ignorance? Science resembles war in many respects: it is a communal venture, with its strategy and tactics of inquiry, often involving bitter conflict between opposing camps but without bloodshed. And what is politics but the continuation of war, except by other means—to reverse the famous dictum of Clausewitz. Even military strategists are coming to see the cold war as a social and economic contest rather than a conflict of armed camps; it is thus that the character of war may be transformed from a destructive to a constructive activity.

March 1964

Does Military Deterrence Deter?

RAOUL NAROLL

In a time when Polaris submarines patrol the seas and Minuteman missiles are poised for flight at the flick of a switch, it sometimes seems as if modern military technology had created an entirely new, uniquely terrifying human situation in which past experience provides no answers to our present dilemma. How could such problems as the "balance of terror" or the credibility of the Strategic Air Command possibly be solved by considerations of military antiquities such as the fire-and-movement tactics of the Iroquois Indians or the exchanges of hostages among the Hottentots? But the waging of war goes back a long way in human culture. The techniques change, but the underlying human propensities for war—and for peace—remain constant.

It is known that primitive tribes—although lacking the destructive capability of civilized peoples—have a wider variety of military practices and warlike attitudes. A know-

29

ledge of how and why primitive peoples made war may shed light on the prospects for war or peace in our own time.

When we sort out all the arguments men make about war and peace—in UN debates, around the Geneva conference tables, in the editorial columns—most of them these days turn out to be variations on four basic theories about the causes and prevention of war:

- the arms race,
- deterrence,
- cultural exchange,
- cultural selectivity.

Each theme has its intellectual proponents who see it as the key to understanding the origins and solutions of the problem of war.

THE ARMS-RACE. This is a favorite theme for many academic authors, the Society of Friends, Ban-the-Bomb petitioners, and White House picketers of various descriptions. The theory holds, simply, that wars are caused by armaments. In an arms race each side strives without limit for military superiority. Neither can be satisfied with simple parity, because an underestimated rival may at any time achieve a technological breakthrough that will give *him* superiority. The psychological climate generated in an arms race is such that each side is likely to interpret the rival's capability as intent: "We are simply protecting ourselves in case of attack, but *they* are arming for war." An arms race thus becomes a circular, self-generating phenomenon of ever-increasing danger. To those who see the problem this way, there are only two possible alternatives—disarmament or annihilation.

DETERRENCE. This theme is most often used in current war/peace literature. Those who have faith in deterrence believe that military preparations can make for peace by vastly increasing the costs of war. A would-be aggressor, in a rational calculation of gain and loss, can be made to realize that the costs of warfare outweigh any possible gain. The advocates of deterrence point out that there is no defense against a nuclear war, and consequently our best hope is for a stable, credible deterrent. For a deterrent to be stable it must be invulnerable so that increased effort against it would be futile. Mutual invulnerability would, from this point of view, stabilize the arms race in a balance of terror. This balance would then, presumably, allow conflicts to shift to limited wars, and to an eventual stabilization and finally to reduction of war.

CULTURAL EXCHANGE. War is simply a large scale case of fear of strangers. Such prejudice against foreigners can be dispelled by first-hand contact, and when contacts increase, war becomes less likely. The exchange enthusiasts attempt to stimulate cultural exchange of every kind. Balletomanes can thank them for the visits of the Bolshoi and Kirov Ballets to these shores, and American actors and musicians can thank them for long-term engagements in the world-wide tours of *Porgy and Bess* sponsored by the State Department. Although such variants of cultural exchange are rather new in human experience, certain kinds of exchange—for example, hostages or wives—have been practiced between rivals for millenia.

CULTURAL SELECTIVITY. War is a basic factor in determining the rise and fall of civilizations. No human society exists alone; it lives with other societies and it must react to threats or be subjugated. Weaker peoples may be eliminated by stronger ones, or their social system radically altered. As societies react to the threats they pose to each other, those traits that make for success in warfare tend to outlast those that do not. This theme is sounded (in language not so anthropological) by those who see current international conflicts as a battle for survival between The American Way of Life and Russian and/or Chinese Communism.

Anthropological studies of primitive societies seem quite remote from such pressing questions of peace or war. What can comparisons of primitive military tactics or the tendency to trade women among Hottentots, Andamans, or Iroquois tell us about the invulnerability of hardened missile sites or military uses of space? While the special circumstances of our own generation, our own decade, this year and next, must obviously dominate the thinking of policy makers, an understanding of the direction in which the deeper currents run can help shape policies with a chance of success over the long term. Let us see what the findings of a cross cultural survey (see box, page 16)—examining the warfare patterns of primitive peoples all over the world—can contribute to the quest for peace in the 1960's.

The two major rival hypotheses about the relationship between armaments and warfare are the *arms race* hypothesis, and the *deterrence* hypothesis. The *deterrence* hypothesis holds that to preserve peace one must prepare for war; in other words, that an orientation to war in a society is inversely related to the frequency of its wars. The *arms race* hypothesis holds that preparation for war tends to make war more likely; thus an orientation to war is directly related to the frequency of war.

We tested these hypotheses by studying the selected cultures for several factors:

■ Warlike traits—such as the possession of guns—that seem to indicate an orientation toward warfare.

■ Frequency of warfare. We divided the cultures into two groups—those where warfare is frequent and those where it is not.

■ Correlations between each warlike trait and the frequency of war. If, for example, all forty-eight cultures in this study have guns, and if they all report frequent warfare, we have found a perfect positive correlation between guns and war. This means that (provided there are no errors in our data) whenever we find a society that has guns, we can predict without a qualm that it is plagued with frequent war. If all forty-eight societies should turn out to have guns and none of them report frequent war, we have found a perfect negative correlation. This means that whenever we encounter a society with guns we will be quite sure that it is rarely troubled by war. If all forty-eight units have guns, and half report frequent wars while the other half do not, then there is no correlation at all; finding that a society has guns won't tell us anything, one way or another, about the likelihood of war. The closer a correlation gets to being perfect the greater the likelihood that reasonable conjectures can be made about other societies possessing similar traits.

These are the warlike traits we finally selected as indications of a military orientation:

- use of fire-and-movement tactics;
- flexibility in the use of surprise tactics;
- multiple expectations of what could be gained by warfare;
- a large number of potential enemies;
- fortifications;
- military preparations other than fortifications;
- boundaries set along the lines of natural obstacles, such as rivers and mountain ranges;
- Western technology, including possession of guns or tools or an expressed interest in firearms;
- expressions of hostility (to test the Freudian theory that if hostility is not expressed within the culture, it will be turned outward in the form of aggression against others).

Some of these traits have subcategories, and nearly all

require some additional explanation.

FIRE-AND-MOVEMENT. According to Harry H. Turney-High's book, *Primitive Warfare: Its Practice and Concepts,* the tactic of first firing on the enemy from a distance and then moving in for hand-to-hand combat is a standard doctrine of modern civilized armies and a characteristic that distinguishes primitive from civilized tactics. The systematic use of fire-and-movement in attack requires a higher degree of coordination and control than the use of either projectiles or hand-to-hand combat alone. This kind of combat is more lethal than simpler tactics and warriors must be specially trained to fight this way. We assumed, then, that a group that uses this tactic is more strongly oriented to war than one that does not.

FLEXIBLE SURPRISE TACTICS. In modern warfare, surprise is a basic tactical principle; the attacker tries to strike his enemy unexpectedly whenever he can. However, surprise is not a universally applied military tactic. Some primitive tribes simply line up at extreme missile range and work up from hurling insults to hurling rocks at each other; this tournament-like war usually ends when the first enemy is killed. This kind of combat is a prearranged tryst, like duels under the European *code duello.* In other tribes, however, the warriors will not fight at all unless they can be sure of taking the enemy by surprise. Tribes like this usually send out raiding parties that lurk near the hostile settlements until they can catch their victims unaware. If the victims are alerted, the attackers simply go home.

The most militarily effective attitude toward surprise, of course, is to seek it but not to insist upon it. We held that societies who were capable of this flexible attitude toward surprise tactics had a stronger military orientation than those that held out for surprise alone or those who stuck to tournaments.

MULTIPLE EXPECTATIONS. An anthropologist, as an observer from the outside, probably cannot say with certainty what the causes of primitive warfare are. However, it is possible for him to make a much simpler and very useful set of observations about what the members of a war party in a particular culture have in mind when they set out for the attack. This "expectations" approach to primitive warfare was introduced by the anthropologist Quincy Wright in an earlier cross-cultural survey. Wright stated that military expectations in primitive tribes occurred in a certain order, such that the first expectation was always present in warfare; the second was never found without the first, nor the third without the other two, etc.

Our study, like Wright's, found that military expectations did occur in a certain order. The scale they formed ran this way:

1. Revenge and defense. Tribes fight to gain satisfaction for injuries (like murder or witchcraft spells), or to expel a foe from their territory. *All* warring tribes have this expectation.

2. Revenge, defense, and plunder. Tribes may also fight, in addition to the expectation above, for booty of some economic value—cattle, wives, slaves, land, cannibal victims (where the whole body, rather than some ceremonial portion, is consumed for food).

3. Revenge, defense, plunder, and prestige. In addition to both expectations above, warriors will go to battle to prove their military prowess—for instance, to acquire scalps or victims for ceremonial cannibalism.

4. Revenge, defense, plunder, prestige, and political control. The incorporation of the defeated enemy into the political system of the victor becomes an additional goal of warfare. Tribes where all of these expectations are in force, we assumed, are more likely to go to war than tribes where

only some of them occur.

MANY POTENTIAL ENEMIES. For each culture unit in the study, we tried to estimate the total number of war-making units which the society might consider to be potential enemies. If a society had more than ten potential enemies, it scored high on this measure; one with less than ten enemies scored low. As this measure actually worked out, the primary contrast was between societies with about five potential enemies and those with more than twenty-five. Our working hypothesis on this point is simply that the larger the number of potential foes, the more likely it is that there will be trouble with at least one of them.

MILITARY READINESS. Societies that carry out routine reconnaissance missions, or regularly post sentinels, or have a customary place for warriors to assemble in case of danger have this trait. We consider its presence an indication of a military orientation.

FORTIFICATIONS. Clearly, societies that build fortifications, like fences or man traps, have warfare in mind.

NATURAL OBSTACLES AS BOUNDARIES. We made the working hypothesis that societies that locate their boundaries along the lines of natural obstacles—like rivers or mountain ranges—were more concerned with the possibilities of warfare than societies that did not.

WESTERN TECHNOLOGY. The possession of guns, Western tools, and/or a lively interest in firearms were taken as indications of war orientation.

REPRESSED HOSTILITY. Societies can express their hostility through malicious gossip or quarreling or public ridicule or insults; a society in this study that did none of these things was considered to have a degree of repressed hostility which might find expression in warfare.

Once these traits of military orientation are defined, the next step in the process is to measure the frequency of war in each unit. Using the writings of ethnographers as sources, we considered warfare to be frequent when they used words like "perpetual," "periodic," "annually," "history of wars and conquests," to describe a culture's warfare involvement. Frequent warfare is absent where such reports say that war is "rare," "unusual," "sporadic," and so on. In the absence of more precise, comparable measurements, we were content to assume that the societies which had references to frequent wars fought more often and more intensively than the other societies.

Now we are ready to look for significant correlations. First let us see how the *frequency of war* is related to the characteristics of military orientation which we have defined.

The first conclusions that emerge clearly from these correlations have to do with deterrence. If the deterrence hypothesis were correct, then societies with strong military orientations would have less frequent war. *This study gives no support at all to the deterrence theory.* Very few of the measures of military orientation seem to have any impact, one way or the other, on the frequency of war. Strong negative correlations, which would support the deterrence hypothesis by demonstrating that war frequency decreases as military orientation increases, are completely absent.

The only significant correlations—*multiple expectations, military readiness, forts,* and *hostility*—are positive, and seem to indicate that these military orientations are positively associated with frequent wars. The strongest relationship that shows up is the positive correlation between *war frequency* and *military expectations*. Since that is so, let us also take a look at the relationships between *military expectations* and the other war-orientation traits:

Military Expectations Correlations

Trait	Strong Positive	Moderate Positive	No Relationship
Fire and movement		+	
Many enemies		+	
Military readiness	+		
Forts	+		
Boundaries			O
Technology			O
Hostility			O

Now let us see how the *frequency of war* is related to the characteristics of military orientation which we have defined:

War Frequency Correlations

Trait	Strong Positive	Moderate Positive	No Relationship
Fire and movement			O
Surprise sometimes			O
Multiple expectations	+		
Many enemies			O
Military readiness		+	
Forts		+	
Boundaries			O
Technology			O
Hostility		+	

The measures of warlike orientation most closely associated with *military expectations* seem to be *military readiness* and *fortifications*. That is to say, societies that expect more kinds of satisfactions from successful warfare tend to be societies which fight more frequently and which make more preparation for war. They also tend to be societies with large numbers of *potential enemies,* that use *fire-and-movement* tactics.

What we are saying, in other words, is that these data offer a kind of mild and tentative support for the arms race hypothesis. However, the positive correlations between war frequency and the two armaments measures—*readiness* and *forts*—are not very large, and they could possibly be a chance result. It is also possible that the existence of *military readiness* and *fortifications* are the *result,* and not the cause, of frequent warfare. The *arms race* remains a possible interpretation of this data, if we see all three variables—war frequency, military preparations, and fortifications—as reflections of an underlying war orientation.

We have subjected the notions of *deterrence* and the *arms race* to a cross cultural test; now let us examine the idea that the significance of warfare is its role as an agent of cultural survival.

No single factor plays the dominant role in the selection of traits in cultural evolution; we know that warfare is one of a number of possible trait-spreading mechanisms. The question that concerns us here is not whether warfare explains everything about cultural selection but whether it plays a part of any consequence at all in deciding which traits are retained and which are dropped. What we are asking here, in contemporary terms, is whether the "American Way of Life" or Communism is more likely to survive and possibly spread if the United States or the Soviet Union and/or China are militarily successful.

In this study we measure the effect of warfare on culture in terms of territorial change. There are a number of reasons for using this measure. If we had chosen to use "success" in warfare, we would have run into the difficulty of defining success in different ways for different cultures.

In some cultures, the pure emotional satisfaction of expressing hostility seems to be the chief object of war. In others, bringing home trophies is the standard. Modern societies, whose wars are fought by professional military men to gain ends defined by professional statesmen (who are usually military amateurs) define success in war in terms of imposing the will of the victorious nation (that is, the will of that nation's statesmen) upon the people of the defeated nation.

If we stick to territorial changes, our task is simpler. For all societies, defense of tribal territory when challenged is seen as a desirable outcome of war. The opposite possibility —the complete loss of tribal territory—can mean the complete extinction of the culture as a distinct way of life. This was the fate of such enemies of the Iroquois as the Neutrals and the Hurons, for example. In the course of recorded history, many highly influential, civilized cultures have perished utterly—their languages forgotten and their political organizations annihilated: this was the fate of the Sumerians, the ancient Egyptians, the Minoan Cretans, the Hittites.

This study indicates that territorial change is usually accomplished by force of arms. Of the fifty societies which we looked at for data on territorial change, twenty-one reportedly had no change during the period recorded (usually the century preceding colonial conquest). Of the twenty-nine that did have changes in territory, only three experienced the change peacefully (and one of these, the Araucanians, posed so great a military threat to its neighbors that one suspects that intimidation, rather than generosity, was responsible for its territorial accretions).

Territorial change, then, is a reasonable measure of the chances of survival of a culture, and such changes are almost always the result of warfare. We used two measures of territorial change: *growth* and *stability*. Both measures consider the ratio of territory the tribe gained or lost during the period studied to the territory the tribe had at the beginning of the period. The *growth* measure also takes into account the direction of the change—territory gained or lost.

The *growth* measure, by itself, would not be sufficient as a measure of cultural survival. The *stability* measure ignores the direction of change. Since territorial change almost always occurs through war, and since the outcome of a war is a very chancy matter, the society that keeps out of war as much as possible and avoids both gains and losses of territory may be the society most likely to survive.

The significant correlations between measures of war orientation, territorial growth, and territorial instability show several important relationships:

■ Territorial growth has a strong positive correlation with Western technology and a moderative positive correlation with military readiness.

■ Territorial instability has a strong positive correlation with military expectations and also a moderate positive correlation with military readiness.

Thus societies whose territories increase are characterized by Western technology and, to a lesser extent, military readiness. The most plausible explanation is that military preparedness tends to make for territorial expansion. The correlations also show a strong tie between territorial instability and military expectations. Societies which hope for a great deal from warfare are societies whose boundaries are likely to change, one way or another. It is tempting to explain this as a three-link chain of influence, with war frequency leading to increased expectations, and increased expectations leading to instability by making tribal land the stakes of warfare. The results here are equivocal, but they do demonstrate that warfare is an agent of cultural selectivity, and that the notion that we can best preserve our way of life by throwing away our arms is dangerously naive.

There is another naive theory of the causes and cures of warfare that is part of our present-day mythology: the theory that wars are simply a kind of prejudice against strangers, and that therefore we can prevent war by getting to know our enemies better. There are certain obvious difficulties with this proposition: in view of the profound value differences now existing between modern nations, it is quite possible that the better we get to know our enemies the more thoroughly we will dislike them. For the time being, however, we will put aside this possibility and subject the cultural exchange theory to our cross-cultural test.

We found useful data on three measures of peaceful intercourse between peoples: subsidies, trade, and women. A subsidy is a payment that one tribe makes to another for the single purpose of assuring a military alliance. When a weak society is paying out sums to a strong one, we think of the transaction as a tribute the weak people pay for the privilege of being left alone. Perhaps as often, however, the money is paid between nations of equal military strength (money flowed from 18th century England to her continental allies like Frederick the Great of Prussia), or from the strong to the weak (as rivers of foreign aid stream out from the US to her allies in the underdeveloped world). By trade we mean an exchange of goods of any kind—including slaves or wives—between potential enemies. Women—whether they are purchased, wooed, or raped—become part of their husband's household; the exchange of women, therefore, represents the most complete form of cultural contact. In many primitive groups men seek wives in communities which are also their potential military foes.

Our comparisons, regretably, show no significant relationships at all between the frequency of war and these three measures of peaceful intercourse.

Our survey of primitive tribes has yielded a number of results that are relevant to current US policy. The study indicates that in the very long run preparation for war does not make peace more likely. It does not seem to make much difference either way, but if it makes any difference at all it is in the direction of making war more likely than peace.

The study shows at the same time that military preparedness in the long run tends to favor territorial growth. Technological innovation seems to be especially effective. This finding supports the common-sense notion that you protect your culture by being prepared to defend it, and is quite incompatible with the position of the unilateral disarmers who claim that a country can best ward off attack by demonstrating its own peaceful intentions. Further study would be necessary to make the results on territorial growth more meaningful. It would be especially useful to identify several types of military preparedness which are substantially unrelated to each other. If territorial growth should prove related to each of these types, the preparedness hypothesis would be very strongly supported indeed.

The findings about military expectations do not have much bearing on current policy, simply because the military expectations of the rival powers today are at their maximum. This is to say that, if war occurs, there appears to be no limit to the kinds of benefits the victor might hope to derive. This is not to deny that both sides to a nuclear exchange might suffer losses far greater than any conceivable gain from victory, but only to state that if one side is clearly victorious in a general war it will not limit its demands upon the survivors of the defeated power.

The findings about peaceful intercourse indicate that it

is not realistic to hope that person-to-person programs will do much to ameliorate the international situation. There may well be other reasons amply justifying such exchanges, but this study can offer no support at all for the idea that they lessen the likelihood of war.

Clearly, more creative approaches to the way peace problems can be solved in the second half of the twentieth century are required if our culture, too, is not be become merely a reference point in a future study of warfare.

January/February 1966

Non-Governmental Organizations

LOUIS KRIESBERG

When the fourteenth World Ploughing Contest was held in Christchurch, New Zealand, in May contestants from every part of the globe arrived to take part. An equally diverse group assembled in Munich last July for the International Dairy Congress. Tokyo will be the scene of the World Road Congress later this year, and the British Paper and Board Makers' International Association of Paper Historians convened in the university town of Oxford in September. Doctors of many nationalities will gather in cities on every continent to discuss recent advances and obstacles in specialized fields of medical research.

Such international nongovernmental organizations (NGO's) now number almost 2,000, compared with fewer than 200 at the beginning of the century. They include groups with interests ranging from bicycling to nuclear physics.

The burgeoning of such organizations is due largely to

the increasing specialization of both work and leisure activities in industrialized societies. Aided by the increasing speed and decreasing cost of international travel and communication, people with special interests are crossing national boundaries more and more often to compare notes and promote common goals in groups such as the International Chamber of Commerce and the International Union of Health Education. With the exception of sharp drops preceding the two world wars and during the early 1950's, the rate of NGO formation has increased steadily.

NGO's may help ease world tensions. Perhaps they are even an index of the extent to which a world society already exists. They foster the development of international perspectives by reinforcing interests that cross-cut national boundaries. Their activities ameliorate the material and social conditions—the hunger, disease, and overcrowding—that underlie certain international conflicts. Formulas for settling international dissension may be developed in them and then incorporated into international law. They may even develop structural arrangements for handling conflicts among their own members that can later be used by governmental organizations such as the UN and its affiliates.

Most NGO's are concerned with occupational activities. Scientists the world over, for example, share interests in better crop yields and the conquest of crippling and killing diseases.

These like or common interests may spur them to joint efforts; and even their national differences may provide the basis for complementary interests and active exchange. But as members of different political systems, the members of various occupational and other kinds of organizations may also have some conflicting interests. This would seem especially likely between Americans and Soviets.

Can Americans and Soviets put aside their enmities to

promote, as members of the same voluntary organizations, common or complementary rather than conflicting interests? Is cooperation—a significant step beyond mere coexistence —really possible? A recent study I made of the nature and membership of NGO's suggests that it is.

About one-third of all NGO's restrict membership to some geographic area. Of the remaining, 21 percent have members from both the U.S. and U.S.S.R., 50 percent from the U.S. but not the U.S.S.R., 3 percent from the U.S.S.R. but not the U.S., and 26 percent from neither. If the generally high U.S. level of participation in NGO's and the very low Soviet level are considered, this means that the U.S. and U.S.S.R. are more likely to be in NGO's with each other than in NGO's in which the other is not represented.

The likelihood of joint membership varies further with the type of organization. NGO's which are made up of workers—for example, trade union organizations—are numerous, but there are few in which both the U.S. and the U.S.S.R. are represented. Such organizations constitute about 10 percent of the NGO's in which the U.S. but not the U.S.S.R. is represented, 14 percent of the ones in which the U.S.S.R. but not the U.S. participates, and 17 percent of the NGO's to which neither the U.S. nor the U.S.S.R. belongs; but they constitute only 1 percent of all the NGO's in which both nations participate. The pattern for NGO's in the area of commerce and industry is similar: 11, 4, 18, and 2 percent, respectively. On the other hand, in science and scientific research, the percentages are quite different: 4, 0, 2, and 18 percent, respectively.

NGO's may be classified in terms of their potential for consensus. The types are intended to reflect the varying degrees to which members of the international community, and particularly the U.S. and U.S.S.R., share goals and beliefs about the means to reach these goals.

■ Type 1 NGO's are concerned with technology, science, medicine, or sports. Consensus is presumably relatively high.

■ Type 2 consists of the social or economic NGO's organized by employer, profession, or trade union; they include groups in commerce and industry, social and political science, law and administration. In these, consensus is presumably moderate.

■ Type 3 includes NGO's dealing with matters about which consensus is presumably low—philosophy and religion, international relations, social welfare, education and youth, and the arts. The arts are included because officially recognized writing, painting, and film-making in the Soviet Union tend to be dominated by the aesthetic of "social realism," a highly idealized depiction of Soviet life that strongly promotes the Soviet ideology.

On the whole, the findings presented in Table I show that the U.S. and U.S.S.R. are most likely to be represented in organizations concerned with matters of presumably high consensus. About half of the NGO's in which they both participate are in the science-health category, while among the organizations in which neither participates, only about one-fifth are concerned with such matters.

In areas in which consensus is high, issues are often viewed as technical matters. Where consensus is low, value differences are likely to be prominent. But as a consideration of organizational structure will show, the extent to which an issue is viewed as a technical or a value matter is not inherent in the issue itself.

Even when Americans and Soviets find sufficient cause to become members of the same NGO's, some areas of conflict inevitably remain. How do organizations with such joint membership keep from being hamstrung by continual dissension? How do they carry out their day-to-day activities so as to minimize potential conflict?

The fact that these organizations often have higher levels of activity than those in which either or both the U.S. and the U.S.S.R. are absent is ample evidence that the former organizations, despite the risk of disruption, do function quite well. They are more likely than the latter to report engaging in activities such as coordinating research; providing services like libraries, abstracting services, and training programs for members; and developing standards or agreements about nomenclature and uniform codes.

The puzzling feature of the situation is that they do so without any relative increase in the size of the organizational staff which might seem necessary for carrying out these operations. This is because, with considerable personnel, the staff or an executive secretary often has relatively great power in the organization's policy formation. The delegation of such power to staff members is not likely to occur in an organization whose members have many conflicting interests—each side fears that the staff is in league with the other. It is not surprising, then, that NGO's with joint Soviet and American participation are somewhat less likely than others to have staffs of ten people or more.

Further decentralization of power in NGO's with joint U.S. and U.S.S.R. participation occurs due to the relative simplicity of organization—that is, the small number of organizational levels. The rank and file are not isolated from the decision-making core by an elaborate superstructure. However, even in the absence of such centralized decision-making, there are few general meetings in which the rank and file can participate directly in policy formation.

Taken together, these findings show some baffling inconsistencies. Joint U.S. and U.S.S.R. participation does not seem to lessen organizational activity, but the development of a large staff to implement this activity may be inhibited. Similarly, an elaborate number of organizational levels may be lacking; but frequent general membership meetings are not substituted to compensate for this structural arrangement. These inconsistencies are partially resolved when we consider one other organizational characteristic: the number of committees in the NGO's.

Despite the jokes about committees and their proliferation, they can be a useful device for organizations. They tend to transform problems from political issues to be decided by bargaining and negotiation to technical matters to be resolved by consensus among experts. Thus, the distinction between technical and nontechnical issues depends largely upon the persons trying to solve the issue and how they handle it, not on the issue itself or on the content area. If the mode of reaching a decision involves logrolling and bargaining and the style of the discussion is polemical debate, the issue will be nontechnical and political. Certain conditions can make such features more prominent. If the participants have clear constituencies who can hear the discussion, if there are many constituencies represented, and if the question is phrased in such broad terms that basic value differences are attached, then the issue is not likely to be viewed as a technical one.

Establishing committees can affect these conditions. Committees meet in relative privacy, and constituents do not hear the discussion. Members of a committee may be selected because of their specialized knowledge—their "expert" qualities; this makes it more likely that they will discuss the issue in technical terms and feel independent of definite constituencies. A small committee limits the number of constituencies involved. Handing problems to a committee usually means first dividing the problem into some of its components, and this makes each component seem relatively technical. And fundamentally, a few persons meeting regularly and frequently can develop rules of

TABLE I—TYPE OF NATIONAL PARTICIPATION IN NGO'S

Type of NGO	U.S. and U.S.S.R.	U.S., but not U.S.S.R.	U.S.S.R., but not U.S.	Neither U.S. nor U.S.S.R.
Science, health, etc.	53	22	18	18
Economic, social, etc.	28	41	43	56
Religion, art, international relations, etc.	19	36	39	26
Total	100	99	100	100

TABLE II—NUMBER OF NGO COMMITTEES BY TYPE OF NGO AND NATIONAL PARTICIPATION

Number of Committees	Science, health, etc.		Economic, social, etc.		Religion, art, international relations, etc.	
	U.S. and U.S.S.R.	Not U.S. and U.S.S.R.	U.S. and U.S.S.R.	Not U.S. and U.S.S.R.	U.S. and U.S.S.R.	Not U.S. and U.S.S.R.
None	52	75	47	64	50	69
1-6	14	5	9	10	11	8
7-10	7	1	4	4	3	2
11 or more	9	1	11	3	6	2
Some, but number not given	18	18	28	19	31	19

discussion and common understandings. The shared understandings diminish value differences.

The number of committees NGO's have is highly associated with whether or not the U.S. and the U.S.S.R. both participate in them. (See Table II) If the U.S. and U.S.S.R. both participate, the NGO is much more likely to have committees than if either or both parties are not represented. Of course, large NGO's tend to have more committees than small NGO's. But even holding the size factor constant, those with joint American-Soviet participation tend to have the most committees.

The use of committees, then, shows ways that organizations can be integrated along international lines and still maintain their activities somewhat independently of the amount of consensus or conflict among their members. It also shows that international give and take—for example, the sort of open exchange that can occur in frequent general membership meetings—must often be limited in order to assure the functioning survival of such organizations. These restraints circumscribe their role in fostering international contact, but NGO's can and do still serve as pilot projects for improving world cooperation.

December 1967

FURTHER READING SUGGESTED BY THE AUTHOR:

Preventing World III: Some Proposals edited by Quincy Wright, William M. Evan, and Morton Deutsch (New York: Simon and Schuster, 1962). See "Transnational Forums for Peace" by Evan, a discussion of ways NGO's contribute to international peace.

International Non-Governmental Organizations by Lyman C. White (New Brunswick, N.J.: Rutgers University Press, 1951). Descriptions of membership in and activities of a variety of important NGO's.

Soviet Sport by Henry W. Morton (New York: Collier Books, 1963). The history of sports activities in the U.S.S.R. and changes in its participation in international events.

The International Labor Movement by Lewis L. Lorwin (New York: Harper and Bros., 1953). The history of changing relations among trade-union organizations of the U.S.S.R., the United States, and the rest of the world.

Yearbook of International Organizations (Brussels, Belgium, Union of International Associations, 1966–67 edition). A comprehensive dictionary of all existing, incipient, and deceased international governmental and nongovernmental organizations, together with information about activities, structure, membership, address, and officers.

Comments on
Report from Iron Mountain

In August of 1963, if we can believe Leonard C. Lewin, a Special Study Group was set up, under Government auspices and with melodramatic secrecy, in order

1. to determine what problems the United States would face if permanent peace broke out; and

2. to draw up a program to deal with these problems.

The Study Group's sponsor was probably an *ad hoc* Government committee at, or near, the cabinet level. Included among the Group's 15 members were an economist, a sociologist, a cultural anthropologist, a psychologist and a psychiatrist, and one literary critic. The 15 met once a month, usually for two days, over a period of two and a half years, the first and final meetings being held in an underground nuclear shelter inside Iron Mountain, in upstate New York (near war-gamer Herman Kahn's Hudson Institute). A report was unanimously agreed upon, then submitted to the Government "interagency committee," along with an urgent recommendation that its contents be kept secret.

There the matter rested—until winter 1966, when a member of the Study Group, "John Doe," came to New York, looked up Leonard Lewin, and handed him a copy of the report, explaining that while he himself accepted all of the *Report*'s conclusions, he also strongly believed that its findings should be made public. Lewin promptly found a publisher, wrote an introduction, included an interview with John Doe, and refused to say another word about the report's origins.

Report from Iron Mountain on the Possibility and Desirability of Peace, with Introductory Material by Leonard C. Lewin (The Dial Press, New York, 1967) says, in essence, that while permanent peace may be possible, it probably would not be desirable. To quote the *Report*: "It is uncertain, at this time, whether peace will ever be possible. It is far more questionable, by the objective standard of continued social survival rather than that of emotional pacifism, that it would be desirable even if it were demonstrably attainable."

Peace, the *Report* concludes, is hell. If society is to remain stable, wars must continue. "War itself is the basic social system, within which other secondary modes of social organization conflict or conspire." The indispensable functions that war and war preparedness serve are assigned to various categories, perhaps the key ones being economic, political, sociological, and ecological.

1. *Economic.* Military spending, by virtue of its independence from the normal supply-demand economy, acts as a balance wheel. "It is, and has been, the

essential economic stabilizer of modern societies." Among possible substitutes offered are a comprehensive social-welfare program; a fantastically elaborate disarmament-inspection system; and an even more enormous investment in space research. Social-welfare programs, however, would not, in the long run, eat up enough resources, and in addition would not remain very long outside the normal economy. A disarmament-inspection system would also not prove "wasteful" enough, and would be incongruous in a world permanently at peace. Space-research programs, the *Report* decides, appear to be the only realistic substitute. (It is the *only* substitute the Study Group warmly endorses.)

2. *Political.* It is only because of the threat of war that individual nations, and stable governments, can exist. ". . . 'war' is virtually synonymous with nationhood. The elimination of war implies the inevitable elimination of national sovereignty and the traditional nation-state." Furthermore, military spending serves to keep a certain portion of the population poor, thus maintaining "necessary class distinctions" and a ready supply of unskilled labor. As a possible substitute, new external enemies might be created—like invaders from outer space, "fictitious alternate enemies," or air and water pollution (which would have to be deliberately intensified). According to the *Report,* only the creation of "fictitious alternate enemies" offers any promise.

3. *Sociological.* The army and the draft serve to remove antisocial members from society. War itself catharsizes aggressive impulses. And the existence of an external menace induces citizens to become patriotic and subservient to the state. "Allegiance requires a cause; a cause requires an enemy." Possible substitutes: programs like the Peace Corps; "Socially oriented blood

games"; and "A modern, sophisticated form of slavery." Of the substitutes, only slavery, the *Report* concludes, may prove "efficient" and "flexible."

4. *Ecological.* War has been the chief evolutionary mechanism for maintaining a proper balance between the population and the supplies the population needs to survive. Here, at least, war has a drawback: It is not eugenic. Nuclear wars, for example, kill off the superior as well as the inferior. A possible substitute *and* improvement: ". . . a universal requirement that procreation be limited to the products of artificial insemination," along with "A comprehensive program of applied eugenics."

What the *Report* does, then, is to legitimize war. The Special Study Group's key conclusion is: "If it were necessary at this moment to opt irrevocably for the retention or dissolution of the war system, common prudence would dictate the former course."

The bulk of the available evidence suggests that the book is a hoax. As for the perpetrator, nominees have included Richard Rovere, John Kenneth Galbraith (who told *Trans-action,* archly, "If I had been a member of the Study Group, I would have been sworn to secrecy"), Kenneth Boulding (whose *Disarmament and the Economy* is quoted), Vance Bourjaily, and— anticlimax of anticlimaxes—Leonard Lewin. All roads, however, lead to Leonard Lewin: he is a freelance journalist who has reviewed a book on think-tanks, he edited *A Treasury of Political Humor,* and he loaned a working draft of the *Report* to a *Trans-action* informant.

The *Report* is far from being "just a hoax," though, and it cannot be dismissed out of hand. Despite its many specious arguments and its spotty knowledge of social science, it is also an acutely accurate satire. What it satirizes is explained by John Doe: ". . . what they wanted from us was a different kind of *thinking*. It was a matter of approach. Herman Kahn calls it 'Byzantine' —no agonizing over cultural and religious values. It is the kind of thinking that Rand and the Hudson Institute and [the Institute for Defense Analysis] brought into *war* planning. . . ." War-gaming has become peace-gaming.

The fact is that the *Report* could have been compiled entirely from authentic sources. There are many social scientists doing this kind of investigation; there are members of the Defense Department who think like this. As one reader has observed, "This provides a better rationale of the U.S. Government's posture today than the Government's official spokesmen have provided. A better title for the book, in fact, would have been the same as Norman Mailer's novel: *Why Are We in Vietnam?*"

The threat that the *Report* holds is not so much that it will be believed and acted upon, but that it *has* been believed and acted upon. Significantly, *Trans-action* has found that those readers who take the book seriously tend to be Government officials. Upon inquiry, sources very close to the White House were authorized to say that the files and libraries of the Executive Office of the President have been reviewed, and although some reports in the general subject area covered by the *Report* were found, there was no record of this particular report. These sources believed, therefore, that no comment was appropriate at this time. Informally, they observed that their statement does not rule out the possibility that the *Report* was sponsored either in the White House, by some Congressional committee, or by some other agency within the Federal Establishment.

More important than the need to know whether *Report from Iron Mountain* is authentic or not, the public needs to know what the current thinking of U.S. Government agencies is in regard to (1) what problems the United States would face in the event of peace and disarmament and (2) what programs should be devised to deal with these problems.

One Defense Department informant has admitted that some of his colleagues have agreed with the *Report*'s conclusion that the Vietnam war is sound because at least it helps preserve stability at home. Another informant, who works at the highest levels in strategic planning within the Pentagon, asserted after reading the *Report* that he saw no reason to consider it a hoax, since he often comes upon reports that read in much the same way. Yet a third person—a recent alumnus of the defense Establishment—found the *Report* quite credible. All this testifies to the enormous gap between secret Governmental assessments of questions of war and peace, of disarmament, and of the "war system" and official public stances—as much as it testifies to Mr. Lewin's skill as a creator of social-science fiction.

The publication of *Report from Iron Mountain,* whatever its source, should become an occasion for a new public demand for a penetrating examination and evaluation of Government reports on strategic planning for disarmament and peace. The extent to which a belief in the desirability and inevitability of "the war system" is built into the operational conceptions of the Government is of deepest public concern, not to be thwarted by claims that these are matters of state that require secrecy.

Irving Louis Horowitz

HENRY S. ROWEN

The most interesting aspect of the *Report* is the reaction to it in the press and among reviewers. It has been described as "original," "acute," "skillful," "chilling," "genuine." It is none of these. It is superficial and lacking in bite. That it should create a certain commotion is, perhaps, more a reflection on the generally low level of public discussion on matters of strategy, international affairs, and disarmament than anything else.

The consequences of disarmament or, to use the terminology of the *Report,* the abandonment of the "war-system" is certainly a subject worthy of serious discussion. So it is conceivably worthy of satire. After all, the U.S. Government supports the objective of general and complete disarmament. If that state of affairs, however it might be defined, were to be brought about, it would certainly be associated with a profound change in relations among states and even within them. And given the variety of opinions to be found in our society, there may be some people who hold a position resembling that presented in the *Report.* Evidently some reviewers think so. But for most of the arguments put forward in the *Report,* I can find little substance in fact, nor can I identify the advocates of the view held.

Statements such as "An economy as advanced and complex as our own requires the planned average annual destruction of not less than 10 percent of gross national product . . . ," or "As an economic substitute for war [a social program] is inadequate because it would be far too cheap," or "the rate of pollution could be increased . . ." in order to have an enemy to fight, or the suggestion that slavery be reintroduced to our society in order to maintain social control, are not ludicrous versions of serious views; they are merely ludicrous.

Most of the *Report* deals with the social and economic effects within the nation state of general and complete disarmament. The *Report* has little to say about the international consequences of disarmament. Here it has largely overlooked what those who "commissioned" the *Report* might have expected as an essential topic for discussion. It is characteristic of the casual nature of this work that it fails to cite Tom Schelling's original and important observations on the consequences of "total" disarmament and to deal with the issues he raises. (Thomas C. Schelling, "The Role of Deterrence in Total Disarmament," *Foreign Affairs,* April 1962.)

Finally, the *Report* would have a greater effect if it had more of the marks of a genuine, Establishment-commissioned product. The little things—concessions, references to contemporary international affairs, hedges, touching of the bureaucratic bases—are largely missing.

ANATOL RAPOPORT

The consensus among reviewers is that *Report from Iron Mountain* is a hoax. But how can one tell the hoax from the real thing these days? There are, of course, the give-aways, the thinly veiled satirical allusions; but what if these were deleted? Satire makes a point if certain aspects of the situation satirized are magnified to grotesqueness. Thus *Doctor Strangelove* was a satire, because there the life of the planet depended upon the availability of 55 cents to put into a pay telephone. But what is there in the *Report* that stretches credibility?

Recall that when *On Thermonuclear War* first came out, the late James R. Newman refused to believe in its authenticity. Now we know better. The barrier of the Unthinkable has been breached once and for all.

Well, not quite. It has been breached on one side only and remains as solid as ever on the other. If the valiant souls who dare look into the abyss were really daring, they would find charming solutions for some of the most tantalizing problems that they pose.

Take one of the principal theses of the *Report,* namely that the continued existence of war or, at least, of the war machine is essential to the health of an advanced economy and to the integrity of a society. Grant the thesis. Now what is wrong with this solution: All war production continues and even expands, as the needs of the economy demand; but the products are declared obsolete immediately instead of in two or three years, which is presently the case? Consequently the products are destroyed as quickly as they are produced. Not only is employment not curtailed but it is actually expanded by the added demolition personnel. Also storage space is saved.

It may be objected that this procedure amounts to disarmament. However, as long as we are in the realm of the Unthinkable, let us pursue the implications, as befits rational beings. Let us not chicken out. Objections to disarmament are of two sorts, namely the obvious ones, derived from conventional wisdom, and the sophisticated ones, outlined in the *Report.* Now the latter have been disposed of by the proposed solution. Disarmament can be accomplished with full war production undisturbed. As for the other objections, these too can be met.

Why not agree with our potential enemies to exchange military and strategic personnel, each side to do with the personnel so delivered as they see fit? This may be formally equivalent to having each side extend its disarmament to include software as well as hardware, and is therefore subject to the same objections as hardware disarmament. Psychologically, however, the procedure has altogether different overtones. Each side *increases* its security by having the military leadership of the other at its mercy. Thus the mutual distrust and hostility can persist and even grow. The ideological war (necessary, according to the *Report,* to hold society together) can flourish. The military personnel of each side (now hostages) can be subjected to intensive interrogation or can be depleted by a controlled liquidation program. In fact, the whole game of escalation and deterrence can be played on this level.

Here, then, is a program that gives us the opportunity of avoiding the unpleasant by-products of *both* peace *and* war. The constructive and creative aspects of war can go on unimpeded. (Indeed, the reduction of the lag of obsoleteness to zero will stimulate an even more rapid development of war technology.) Nations need not become soft and decadent. The strategists can continue to plot each other's countries' destruction to their hearts' content. Disarmament does not jeopardize the safety of the disarmed nations, since in return for disarmament each gets a chance to deplete the military personnel of its enemies (it need not trust them to do it). The aggressive impulses of man can find an ample outlet on the hostages.

That such proposals were not incorporated in the *Report* speaks for its authenticity.

*   *   *

JESSIE BERNARD

Before commenting on this report, I would like to correct one erroneous rumor. On page XXII, Doe states that "there were no women in the Group." It so happens that I was a member. But my contributions were so contrary to the tenor of the discussions—one blew a fuse when fed into a computer, and computer time was a major expense of the project—that, by consensus, it seemed best for me to drop out. As Doe notes, some of the sessions were rough; we got on one another's nerves. But they wanted a unanimous report, and they ended with no important differences.

I had taken them at their word, namely that they wanted to tackle "the relevance of peace and war . . . to . . . sociological relationships . . . , to psychological motivations, to ecological processes. . . ." But they kept rejecting my suggestions. They wanted to talk about "the antisocial elements," unemployment, social-welfare programs, cultural uplift; I wanted also to talk about the relations between the sexes.

In one session, for example, I pointed out war's emancipating effects on women. I reminded them of the liberating results for women of the Punic Wars, which—taking men away—gave women a great deal of experience in the administration of enterprises. I reminded them that World War I had been followed by the first sexual revolution of this century; women achieved the right to demand orgasm and they also achieved the right to smoke and cut their hair. World War II opened up to women a wide gamut of jobs never before available to them. War, in this sense, was a great plus for women.

But since this point had zero-sum aspects (the war

gains for women often having a minus aspect for men), the Group was reluctant to feed any of it into the computer. They gave as their excuse that they were uncertain as to whether they should feed it in as a cost or as a benefit to the system as a whole.

Finally an answer was provided by Hill, the psychiatrist. War was clearly a plus for men too, for although anything that upgraded women was clearly a cost to the men (he saw all relations between the sexes as zero-sum in nature, in conformity with so much exchange-theory currently fashionable), there was another angle. There were few things, he reminded us, if any, now left exclusively to men. There were even movements afoot to deprive men of the right to buy guns freely. Take war away from them and what did they have left? A line had to be drawn somewhere. The perpetuation of the war system was therefore clearly a benefit to the men, even if it did also incidentally help women.

This was acceptable to the Group until, after a bit of mulling, I reminded them that technology is increasingly depriving men of their monopoly on the war game. As we move more and more in the direction of a push-button war, women can take over quite nicely. Women can sit in the underground war chambers and monitor hostile flights and flying objects as well as men. They can push buttons as easily as men. They can steer unmanned rockets as well as men. In the future, all the really good wars will probably be turned over to women, leaving only the dirty little jungle wars to the men. In the prestigious wars, technology is making it as easy for women to displace men in the war game as in civilian industry. The day might even come, as the President said recently, when there will be a female chief of staff. The very thought of the war system under the control of women was just too much. . . . The horrors of war began to look as intolerable as the horrors of peace. That did it. My presence was so clearly abrasive that I withdrew.

Enough of this. War and peace are too serious to be left to the satirist. Especially to a satirist *manqué* like Doe, who is neither a Swift nor a Veblen nor even a Buchwald. There is not enough bite, not enough sublety, not enough outrage. He strives for wit but achieves only dullness. As a high-level researcher's *revanche* for Congress' ukase of some years back forbidding the inclusion of a "surrender" option in any defense research, it is fairly successful. As a *reductio ad absurdum* of the systems approach, it passes. As a spoof of the sociological functional tradition of the 1950s, which traced the function of every aspect of social systems (crime, ignorance, prejudice, corruption—the list is almost endless), it is a good try. But as the vehicle for "a serious and challenging effort to define an enormous problem" (xv), it is not nearly good enough.

The great overriding point he has is epitomized in the newspaper report, "Wall Street was shaken yesterday by news of an apparent peace feeler from North Vietnam. . . ." Although this may be viewed as only a modern variant and updating of the old Nye investigation of munitions-makers, there is a new angle that is crucial, namely that the "munitions-makers" have now become the great military-industrial complex that President Eisenhower warned us about. A large segment of the economy depends on the military-industrial complex. Peace, in fact, does threaten it, and many of our own perquisites along with it.

I fault the author's judgment in using the anonymity dodge. Instead of focusing discussion on the points he is trying to make, this posture will deflect it to the question of whodunit. A trivial question in comparison with the question he raises: Is war, as we have always thought, a tool of social systems or, as this book concludes, are social systems the tools of wars?

MARC PILISUK

There are several cogent issues raised by *Report from Iron Mountain*. Among them, the question of whether or not the enterprise is a satirical hoax (and I tend to favor this view) seems to matter least.

The fact is that the enterprise is distinctly reminiscent of the style, procedures, and tone of the new operations-oriented, free-wheeling brainstormers whose product is sold and solicited in policy circles as serious social-science analysis. In fact, the *Report* recalls these brainstormers with sufficient vividness to make us quake with fear about the process that does go on.

The early sections deal with the composition of the Special Study Group, and its indoctrination to answer the question set forth without bias. The method previews one that may soon be improved upon, as follows: Add 250 hours of behavioral-scientist time to seven full-time hardware types, one ex-intelligence man, one international-relations type with government experience, two successful industrialists, a regional planner, an eminent physicist, and a Negro (even if the last, because of the demand, must be rented from Hertz). To promote frankness, lubricate the group with some unspeakable jokes or rudeness. In the first section of the final report, insist that one has cornered the market on objectivity and has been able to transgress, in all subsequent conclusions, the moral sensibilities that hinder other mortals. The technique will eventually be amended to include abbreviated T-group (sensitivity-training) sessions, and will then claim that the participants will thereby have achieved either the equivalent of a psychoanalysis or, at least, the Dhyana of the ancient Buddhists. This emphasis upon gaining a virtual monopoly on truth by the purity of the group's cathartic expurgation, or by its own surprise when it saw the light, is something that distinguishes the possessed individual or group from the skeptical scientist or philosopher. The latter, however forceful about their current beliefs, remain dubious about the ultimate validity of these beliefs.

Because the technique is simple and because it disdains the hard work of the social scientist is not sufficient reason to reject the *Report*'s conclusions. With reference to finding an alternative to war, most serious social-science research, as the *Report* suggests, has been trivial—if not in its relevance or in the validity of its conclusions, at least in the paucity of its attempts to find an adequate answer to the question of why its research is not being put to use. Moreover, since empirical research requires some operational statement of what one is talking about, and studies come easier where the topic is limited in scope, few social scientists ever devote themselves to prolonged analysis of how or why the social system *as a whole* evolves into war or peace. Some serious scholars have written about the economics of disarmament (usually with the conclusion that it is manageable, given a pattern of resource reallocations and planning that is about as impossible as disarmament itself). Psychiatrists, anthropologists, and ethologists have written about aggression and violent war (usually with the conclusion that in man, at least, bloodless forms of hostile behavior and of resolving disputes may be possible). Other social scientists have produced a host of ingenious solutions—international armies, agencies, exchanges, alliances, friendships, detection techniques, and so on—all of which have been explored separately. But it is rare to find anyone brash enough to take on the whole gamut of questions at once. In this, *Report from Iron Mountain* stands out. It covers a broad expanse; refers with some familiarity to relevant literature in several fields; and creates hypothetical projections with the gusto of a first-year student in urban architecture creating a city.

The *Report* contributes some penetrating insights into the system of the think-tank operation. One is the use of consensual validation among like-minded people to replace evidence. "It was hard to figure out who were the liberals and who were the conservatives, or who were hawks and who were doves." Shown here are the limits of American pluralism as a check on military-industrial power. Real power determines not who wins out among various political protagonists, but who decides the smorgasbord of which protagonists or which issues will be considered. A currently circulating definition of a dove is: One who favors the least escalation. If pluralism is to operate, it requires something more than this as a counterpower to military interests.

A second insight into the think tank is the use of computer programs to resolve problems for which gross assumptions must be made (and then forgotten) so that the product can have a ring of scientific jargon that sounds good, or at least incomprehensibly authoritative, when presented in Congressional testimony or in special White House reports. Here the gem is the "peace games" method, described as a computer language with a superior capacity to interrelate data with no apparent common points of reference. The product of this method is illustrated with great poignancy in a footnote that explains the prediction that science could still continue to progress for two more decades after the end of the war system:

"This rather optimistic estimate was derived by plotting a three-dimensional distribution of three arbitrarily defined variables: the macro-structural, relating to the extension of knowledge beyond the capacity of conscious experience; the organic, dealing with the manifestations of terrestrial life as inherently comprehensible; and the infra-particular, covering the conceptual requirements of natural phenomena. Values were assigned to the known and unknown in each parameter, tested against data from earlier chronologies, and modified heuristically until predictable correlations reached a useful level of accuracy. 'Two decades' means, in this case, 20.6 years, with a standard deviation of only 1.8 years. (An incidental finding, not pursued to the same degree of accuracy, suggests a greatly accelerated resolution of issues in the biological sciences after 1972.)"

A third characteristic of the think-tank approach is a willingness to promote the causes of some morally-handicapped diviner of the future of mankind. The strategic framework, unhampered by sentiment, assumes that Machiavellian motivation and violence are not only real, but necessary for the best interests of society. If they lead to a destruction of most of society, so be it: The realist faces this prospect and looks beyond. Just as Herman Kahn can deduce the promising opportunities available in the post-nuclear-attack era, so does *Report from Iron Mountain* speak about the population-control advantages of nuclear weapons. Formerly, wars hurt the species by selectively killing off the strongest of its members. The species is now, fortunately, in for a better deal, according to the *Report,* since nuclear weapons will kill indiscriminately. Of course, the *Report* indicates that this gain in the gene pool may be offset by some genetic damage to the survivors (just as Herman Kahn notes, in *On Escalation,* that a nuclear exchange may produce casualties). But at least the stability of our social system would not be jeopardized by disarmament, withdrawal, idealism, or refusal to play the strategic game.

Behind all this satire, the book contains a provocative analysis of how dependent this country is upon war for the centralized planning and domination of resources and personnel that keep the society from embarking upon radical departures from its traditions. That this central argument is shored up by some apparently unfounded assumptions regarding the significance of killing to the culture, arts, science, and even the existence of social systems does not make the argument less valid. Two years ago I did some research into the military-industrial complex and came to an essentially similar conclusion, namely that American society, as we now know it, could *not* make the accommodations necessary to achieve disarmament reallocations, to achieve assistance of the type needed to avert extensive violence stemming from underdevelopment, or to achieve international jurisdiction of disputes.

If the conclusion that current American society is incompatible with peace is valid, the recommendations one makes still depend upon values. *Report from Iron Mountain* remains true to its asserted heritage of the assumed source of all great values, the war system, and it concludes that peace is not to be obtained or desired. Perhaps the recommendation is prophetic for, beneath the rationalizations and moralisms, American policy does continue to make the choices that make future violent conflict inevitable. Still, there are those among us who follow Jeffersonian values and would recommend instead that it is the American system, rather than peace, that has grown dangerous and unresponsive to our needs. Perhaps the United States, rather than peace, is the appropriate target for revolutionary restructuring. The *Report* is one attempt to hasten this process through exposure.

There is danger as well as promise in such satire. During the fallout-shelter controversy, a brilliant piece appeared in *New University Thought* entitled "On Serving Your Fellow Man." It dealt with the problems of convincing people of the advantages of (and overcoming their aversions to) orderly cannibalism in the food-depleted shelter. The approach ranged from the problem of ethics (serving the greatest number with the fewest number) to the problems of appetite (better recipes and prestige-advertising inducements). It was, unfortunately, no more absurd in its rationale than any other part of the shelter program. But I shuddered at the time to think that some secret Special Study Group —imbued with dedication and freed from emotional or moral compunctions—might pick up the suggestion and immediately engage in the technical problem of how to promote this new dimension in shelter living.

We have come a long way when the existing think tanks can plan for levels of genocide matter of factly and with only an occasional need even for secrecy. The *Report* stirs revulsion only in those who play the game in which people count. For the strategy theorists, and that may by now include too many of us, I fear that they have just picked up a trick or two that they might otherwise have missed.

I have been asked twice now whether I wrote the book. I did not. Anatol Rapoport, Kenneth Boulding, Noam Chomsky, Paul Goodman, Donald Michael, Amitai Etzioni, and Irving Horowitz are candidates whose wit, competence, and devotion to peace make them suspect. My great hope, however dim, is that it was done by some dropout from the RAND Corporation as an overture to his reentry into the family of man. My great fear is that the strategic framework of thought is so prevalent and so compatible with the competitive advantage of an affluent society that the *Report* describes a process of controlling the future that is too far along for warnings to be of value.

KENNETH E. BOULDING

I have been publicly accused of writing this book. I did not write it, and I knew nothing about it until I received a page proof, somewhat indirectly, from the publisher. Furthermore, I regard the suggestion that I wrote it as very close to being an insult. If the book is intended as a satire, as it may be, it is written with too straight a face to be wholly convincing. If it is "straight," it represents a point of view that I reject on both intellectual and moral grounds.

Intellectually, the work is clever pinchbeck, operating at the level of popularized folk science. Its economics is folk economics, in spite of the fact that it quotes *Disarmament and the Economy*. The author, or authors, of the work do not understand the significance of economic models and completely underestimate the flexibility of the American economy and its adjustability to any level of military or governmental expenditure.

The basic intellectual fallacy of the book, however, goes far deeper than its particular misunderstandings. It might be called the "functional fallacy." This is the fallacy of supposing that because something exists there must be a good reason for it. Thus, the world-war industry, as I have called it, exists at a certain level, say approximately 10 percent of the gross world product. There must be a reason for this, the book argues, and if the world-war industry were done away with, something specific would have to take its place.

This crude functionalism neglects what is the most important characteristic of social systems—that they operate on a loose dynamic with strong random elements and many degrees of freedom, and that their properties at any one time are simply the result of these loose dynamic processes up to that date. In other words, many things exist for which there are no good reasons at all, but simply because the dynamics of the system produce them. More specifically, many things exist for which there are no good reasons in human welfare, and the world-war industry is one of them. It exists because of a perverse dynamic and it can be done away with by changing the dynamics of the system.

Morally, the work, if "straight," is highly sinister. It is an attempted justification and legitimation of the war industry, and especially of the American war industry, at a moment when the institution of war is threatened with delegitimation because of its outrageously negative payoffs. What is attempted here is a legitimation of the military system, not in the ancient terms of courage and drama that have so largely been drained out of it, thanks to air power and the mass murder of civilians, but in terms of "peace" imposed by universal terror and oppression.

I console myself, however, with the reflection that the dynamics of legitimacy are very complex and that sophisticated attempts to create legitimacy frequently backfire. I am frankly interested in delegitimizing the war industry, and in spite of the fact that I suspect this document had the opposite intention, it may well turn out that its effect will be to further this delegitimization. The reaction may well be, "If this is how the war industry has to be justified, there must be something even more wrong with it than we think." In its results, therefore, this book may turn out to be on the side of the angels.

MURRAY WEIDENBAUM

From the newspaper articles alone, I could not figure out why Mr. Lewin modestly wished to cloak his work in semi-anonymity. A reading of the volume clears up that question rapidly. If this string of unsupported assertions and social-science fiction had been offered under his own name, it would have been laughed off the market as the malevolent musings of an uninformed crackpot.

I particularly regret seeing the numerous factual and analytical errors included in the sections dealing with economics. The general reader is likely to be hard put to separate fact from fiction. For example, "The Special Study Group" repeats the tiresome Marxian cliché that the Vietnam war was stepped up in 1965 "in the usual coordination . . . with dangerously rising unemployment rates." How should the general reader be expected to know that the truth of the matter was just the opposite? Unemployment rates—and total unemployment—were falling all through 1965 *prior* to the Vietnam buildup during the middle of the year. The unemployment rate was 5.2 percent in 1964. It declined from 5.0 percent in February 1965 to 4.5 percent in July 1965. It is hard to believe that such basic distortion of the truth is not malevolent.

Perhaps a more fundamental flaw is the author's contention that the economic and fiscal tools of Federal budget policy would not be effective enough to facilitate the shift of resources from military to civilian uses. The discussion here (page 21) is particularly illogical. First the reader is told that fiscal tools "can provide new incentives in the economy." In the very next sentence, the author states that these tools "reflect the economy; they do not motivate it." (My colleagues in sociology tell me that the sociological sections of *Iron Mountain* are poor, but that the economics chapter seems to be convincing. I will leave to the psychologists the analysis of how to con academics via "interdisciplinary" research.)

Any student of Economics 1 knows that government purchases of goods and services are indeed a source of "final" demand, that the Federal Government's buying of tables or chairs or post-office buildings or space satellites motivates private production and employment just as directly as private customers do. Witness the substantial shift of resources from civilian output to meet the needs of the Vietnam war.

Incidentally, this large and rapid shift of resources also belies the alleged geographical "inflexibility" of military production. The step-up in the Vietnam war has resulted in major shifts in the geographic, industrial, and occupational distribution of military purchasing in the American economy. While some Midwestern states have seen their military contracts double during the last few years, during the same period several of the far Western states—Washington, Utah, and Colorado—have had their defense orders virtually cut in half.

The industrial shifts in military demand during the last few years have been equally dramatic and belie the author's statement that "rigid specialization . . . characterizes modern war production." While the large aerospace and electronics firms have been obtaining declining shares of the military market, clothing and textile orders are up 240 percent, automotive vehicles are up 80 percent, and food is up 60 percent. Details are contained in *Economy Effect of Vietnam Spending*, Joint Economic Committee (Washington, G.P.O., 1967, 2 vols.).

Perhaps the greatest disservice that *Iron Mountain* renders is to lower the level of argument in the crucial dialogue on the prospects for peace. Until now the debates have centered mainly on different interpretations of a common factual basis. We are now reduced to the lower-level chore of cleaning up Lewin's literary litter before it pollutes the intellectual environment. Under the circumstances, it is unfortunate that *Iron Mountain* is receiving greater academic attention than its spiritual ancestor, that earlier anonymous and allegedly suppressed committee report, the *Protocols of the Elders of Zion*.

LEONARD J. DUHL

Whether this book is a hoax or not is irrelevant. What is important is the fact that it exists, and that it reflects a particular style of thinking.

Report from Iron Mountain serves a useful function in pointing out that a peacetime society needs new kinds of social planning to deal with the special problems created by peace. But the book points out this need with that type of long-range thinking that treats ecological models—models that incorporate demographic and geographic variables as well as sociological ones—as completely closed, almost fully controllable, rigid systems.

Irving Louis Horowitz has suggested that fascists use ecology as a model because it gives them their excuse for massive control—for control not just of matters we usually consider the legitimate concerns of government, but of matters (such as who will have children and who will not) that democratic systems consider the business of their individual citizens. An ecological model need not serve such fascistic ends, however. Treated as an open system, an ecological model for social planning can actually help ensure the survival of democratic procedures during the critical adjustments that our society will have to undergo, now and in the future, in order to adapt itself to a state of peace.

The essential fault of the *Report* is its failure to recognize (1) that planning from an ecological model, whether for war or peace, is a *process*—rather than the establishment of a set of rigid systems, and (2) that this process is not oriented toward stability, but toward change.

Our economic, sociological, ecological, cultural, and scientific concerns are concerns for those processes that permit change to occur in each system. The overall social system we seek to preserve is not what the *Report* calls "the survival of the social system we know today." Nor is it based solely upon a set of institutions for which "substitute" institutions must be created. Rather, it is a fluid system composed of changing institutions and processes through which we seek to enable every individual to control and affect the events that control his life.

If one views the problem of peace as an issue we must face, as the *Report* does, one must then give high priority to domestic concerns. And these concerns extend beyond the static and negative one defined by the *Report* as "the survival of social systems we know today." They are, instead, the development of new social systems—and modifications of existing ones— to permit the kind of domestic processes that will enable us to solve our internal problems without turning into a fascistic, controlled, or militaristic state. They require changes toward improvement, rather than merely viewing the stability of society as the "one bedrock value that cannot be avoided."

Certainly the two poles may be anarchy and control. But the planning procedures needed to ensure that our peacetime social system is between these two poles are not those that maximize the value of stability, but those concerned with creating mechanisms to guarantee that the values we hold dear to our society are maintained. How to create these mechanisms so that we can further human development, achieve health, and maximize citizen participation in those events that affect our lives—these are the important questions to which all else must be directed. And these are the questions that the *Report* fails to ask.

A peacetime society in which these mechanisms exist may not be perfectly stable and free of tensions. But social tensions are not war. Society can prepare itself for the tensions accompanying the negotiations for change that permit a society to be viable and active.

That social scientists would permit themselves to become party to a fascistic goal, as they have if this *Report* is real, truly requires that they reexamine their goals for our society. Years ago Kurt Lewin, in *Resolving Social Conflicts* (Harper & Row, 1948), said:

"it seems to be crucial for the problems of social science that the practitioner understand that through social science and only through it can he hope to gain the power necessary to do a good job. Unfortunately, there is nothing in social law and social research which will force the practitioner towards good. Science gives more freedom and power to both the doctor and the murderer, to democracy and Fascism. The social scientist should recognize his responsibility also in respect to this."

Report from Iron Mountain illustrates that the social scientist must reexamine any tendencies he has to define what is good as what is static and structured. It reveals how an ecological model can be twisted into a highly institutionalized and status-quo-oriented approach that negates the essence of ecology—change, and the participation of all segments of a system in the processes through which that change occurs.

BRUCE M. RUSSETT

That some people have accepted Leonard Lewin's cover story for *Report from Iron Mountain* illustrates how easy any government's job really is much of the time— some people will believe *anything*. It also illustrates

once again the risks of satire. Ridicule often fails because some people have no sense of the ridiculous. To
this reader at least, it is apparent that the *Report* is a
spoof, if not on the whole a very funny one. It has to
be a spoof simply because it is presented as the product
of a handsomely-supported team that took a broad,
general, long-term look at the most basic problems of
American foreign policy. Anyone who knows our leaders also knows how small a government audience such a
report would have. Virtually every official is totally im-
mersed in day-to-day problems, though perhaps an
occasional Nostradamus is assigned the task of maintaining a six-month horizon.

That some people have taken the *Report* at face value
makes me worry even more than usually about the
quality of the American debate on foreign policy. Much
of its humor is black, with the best morsels reserved for
the footnotes. My preferred tidbits are the allegedly-
computerized projections based on the "peace games"
computer language, replete with high orders of precision in probability levels, means, and standard devia-
tions, all derived from "arbitrarily defined variables"
where "values were assigned to the known and unknown in each parameter." Anyone who doesn't know
that this is a put-on is a very sad victim of two-culture
isolation.

But of course the truly sad part is that so very many
people cannot recognize put-ons, as is evidenced by the
only slightly more subtle hoaxes perpetrated in many
real prognostications. Too many studies have used
complicated procedures to "analyze" material that was
little more than arbitrary assumptions rather than data.
Similarly, the *Report* is a spoof of documents that state
complicated conclusions about social reality as simple

assertions, buttressed only by supreme confidence and an illustrative aside about the organization of the Inca empire. This sort of thing requires me to affirm, varying a famous question and answer, that there is *not* a John Doe.

Other victims of the satire, besides the hardnosed "strategic thinkers," are the peaceniks who have not understood the system they are trying to transform. Here the author(s) of the *Report* rise(s) above the style of gay potshots to warn us of the intractability of the war system—for me, one of the book's two serious purposes is to suggest just how hard it would indeed be to institute permanent peace. Those who would abolish war must examine their own unsupported assumptions, and do a kind of careful, massive, detailed research job that has never been attempted, and for which we have little more than the fraudulent substitutes parodied by this book.

Finally, the book seems to be most centrally concerned with the consultants and officials who "avoid" value judgments in their rigorous pursuit of deduction to objective conclusions unhindered by bias. In fact, the values of the putative authors are pervasive—stability is their highest goal. They are unwilling to take any risks to change the system or to revise the functions that the system serves; they seek survival without caring *what* survives. This unconcern with the *purpose* of America by those who guide its policies is the tragedy of our country and our profession. Perhaps it is because this syndrome is so familiar that so many readers did not recognize the put-on.

January/February 1968

The Failure of Fail-Safe

JOHN R. RASER

"We have defiled our intellect by the creation of such scientific instruments of destruction that we are now in desperate danger of destroying ourselves. Our plight is critical and, with each effort we have made to relieve it by further scientific advances, we have succeeded only in aggravating our peril. As a result, we are now speeding inexorably toward a day when even the ingenuity of our scientists may be unable to save us from the consequences of a single rash act or a lone reckless hand upon the switch of an uninterceptible missile"
General of the Army Omar N. Bradley, Nov. 5, 1957

Every man—whether poet or pimp, philosopher or philanderer—likes to believe that the work to which he applies his energies is of some value. He may define that value in any number of ways: It uplifts the spirit of man, it serves basic human cravings, it increases man's comprehension of the universe, or it fulfills his own indisputable drives. Most of us, lauding consistency more than living it, claim all of the above things at some time, and rationalize our work in terms of any or all of the named values. And like Jeremy Bentham, or like Max Spielman in John Barth's novel *Giles Goat Boy,* we are likely to measure our work by "examining each moment whether what we are doing just now is likely to add to, or detract from, the sum of human misery." It's a tricky and uncertain rule, but it may be the best we can find.

Students of human behavior—behavioral scientists —have special problems in these areas, both because what we study (humankind) is the most precious and volatile element in our world, and because what we discover in our studies can have such a potent effect on the destiny of the very object of study—human beings. Because the study of human behavior is so crucial, and so poorly understood, I should like to outline what behavioral scientists do.

Briefly, we try to understand how human beings act in a variety of situations, by studying them in laboratories and clinics, by using interviews and questionnaires, and by examining historical cases. Some of us go a step further. We interpret what we have learned and apply it to problems of human existence—childrearing, marital relations, racial tensions, poverty, the population explosion, educational policy, or war.

It is this last—war—that is my major interest, and that I wish to discuss. I should like to report on several studies of what happens to human beings in a crisis, then apply the findings of those studies to some aspects of modern warfare. In doing so, I have two objectives. First, I hope to demonstrate that those of us who engage in these difficult and frequently maligned analyses of human behavior sometimes have good reason to believe that our work *is* of value and *does* contribute to the alleviation of human misery; and second, I hope to furnish insights into the crucial role that various assumptions about human behavior can have upon questions of the design of weapons and upon modern military strategy.

I should like to begin by summarizing the findings of several research projects. The first, by James A. Robinson, a professor of political science at Ohio State University, is "Simulating Crisis Decision-Making." The second, "Crises in Foreign Policy Making: A Simulation of International Politics," is by Charles F. Hermann of Princeton University. The third, written at Stanford by Ole R. Holsti, is "Perceptions of Time and Alternatives as Factors in Crisis Decision-Making." The last is a book by physiological psychologist Walter Cannon, *Bodily Changes in Pain, Hunger, Fear and Rage.*

Now, these are jaw-breaking titles and it is obvious from just listing them—without reference to their contents, which are larded with graphs, tables, and formulas—that this is not the type of literature that one keeps on one's coffee table for light reading. Nor are they the kind of document likely to be found in a Congressman's briefcase, a President's chambers, or a general's quarters. But they *are* worth knowing about.

The first two, by Robinson and Hermann, are reports of a complicated laboratory experiment in which military officers acted out the roles of national and military decision-makers in "games" of international affairs. The experimenters introduced crises into the games at various stages—crises that suddenly confronted the officers with intense threats to the achievement of their goals. In studying the officers' behavior in such crises, the experimenters were able to determine that, as a crisis became more intense, the men lost some of their ability to evaluate information, were able to consider fewer alternative courses of action, and tended to be less flexible. In short, as threat increased and time for response decreased, their ability to cope with the situation was lessened.

Holsti's study applied a sophisticated technique of computer analysis to the six-weeks'-long period preceding the outbreak of World War I. His study of the pattern of message flow, and his analysis of the contents of the messages, show plainly that as the crisis intensified, the key governmental and military decision-makers of Austria-Hungary, Germany, England, France, and Russia responded in the same manner as the officers in Robinson and Hermann's laboratory experiment. The decision-makers saw fewer alternatives, they distorted their position in relationship to others, their messages became more stereotyped, and they began to lose the ability to think in long-range terms, focusing their attention instead on extricating themselves from the current problem—and damn the long-range consequences. Thus, as threat intensified, their ability to think and act rationally degenerated, as was true of the officers in the laboratory study.

These studies are among the most recent analyses of the effects of a crisis on decision-making in international relations. Other studies indicate that in most areas of human concern—child-rearing, domestic relations, driving, business, and, indeed, all human activity—conditions of crisis generate similar effects. Panic, terror, hysteria, confusion, anger, and even merely "being rattled" or "upset" can produce these lapses in a person's mental ability. According to the late Harry Stack Sullivan, even the mildest forms of a crisis create

" . . . a considerable degree of imperception, an arrest of constructive, adaptive thinking, and a high degree of suggestibility to almost anything that seems simple and a way out of the difficult situation. There is complete insensitivity to elaborate, difficult suggestions; but the person is relatively impotent to ward off or to resist any simple idea that is given to him."

The point to keep in mind from these three studies, then, is that in times of crisis one is just not able to function as well mentally as one normally does.

The book by Walter Cannon records over 40 years of research on people from several races and cultures. When fear or anger are aroused, he reports, our bodies change. Adrenaline shoots into the bloodstream, the heart speeds up and pumps faster, the muscles expand, the nerves and muscles in the back tense, blood sugar increases, and strength becomes measurably greater. In brief, when faced with a sudden threat, people become—physically—superb fighting machines, far more capable of meeting that threat than otherwise—*if the threat is immediate and physical, and if physical violence is needed to counter it!* Like a cornered rat suddenly transformed into a screeching bundle of fury, launching itself with bared teeth at a man 100 times its size, a desperate and afraid human being turns into a frightening engine of destruction. But as Cannon also points out, while the body gorges itself with strength on account of fear, the mind loses its focus. We think less clearly, we lose our perspective, vision becomes centered on the source of our fear—we are "in a blind rage." Like the rat, we may launch ourselves against an overwhelming adversary, only to go down in "glorious" defeat.

These studies, then, give us a picture supported by much other research. Threat, fear, and rage (crises) *stimulate* us physically but *impair* our mental powers. That's the way we are built, that's how the evolutionary process has coded our glands to operate.

Now I want to change the subject momentarily and discuss the nature of war. Not its value or morality, but its nature. I simply want to describe what it has been like to fight in a war, and how this has changed as we have created sophisticated weaponry to serve our dreams and fears.

Centuries ago, men fought on foot or from horseback, from behind walls and towers. They fought with clubs, knives, spears, swords, bows and arrows, slings, and axes. The Greek or the Hun charged into battle with his every cell inflamed with rage, his heart pounding, adrenaline surging through his veins, his muscles bulging. The defender, too, crouching in his fortress or dashing for his weapon, was suddenly hit with terror, and then rage as he saw the slaughter begin, and he too was transformed into a madly fighting animal. For both, their physiological responses served them well, and their heroic actions became the stuff of epic literature.

More recent developments in weapons mean that the combatants often face one another with guns and flaming jellies. When the man in the trench is suddenly shaken by an exploding shell, or watches his friend's face shattered by a well-placed bullet, rage hits him, his body responds, and his thinking blanks. Screaming vengeance, he may charge suicidally into a hail of machine-gun fire, or dash to toss a grenade into a gunnery nest, or singlehandedly disarm a tank with stones or Molotov cocktails. Again, occasional success is the result. More often, on account of such new death-dealing devices, the outcome is horrible death. Man's instinctual reactions are beginning to conflict with his own cleverness in creating weapons—and are serving him less well. But usually only a few die, so, such incidents, while sad, are probably not important in the scheme of the universe.

But with some types of modern weapons, infinitely greater power has been placed in the hands of the individual. The strategic-bomber pilot over Germany or North Vietnam with his load of TNT or napalm, winging towards his industrial or military target, con-sults a hundred instruments, a dozen charts, groggily remembers a morning briefing, co-ordinates his crew. Now the defenders react—fighters dive from above, flak and missiles ascend from below. Fear clutches the pilot's heart, rage clouds his vision, he is less able to think clearly, he forgets his information, he tries des-perately to get out of trouble—his pounding heart, pulsing veins, and tense muscles are not an aid to him at all, but a hindrance, while his impaired mental power makes him a less, not more, effective fighting man. The result may be, and often is, a blanket of death dumped in fury or error on an innocent hamlet, an empty field, or on the pilot's own troops. No longer is the man whose reasoning power collapses in a crisis the only one to suffer; now others must pay the price. And if the man whose judgment falters under pressure is not a bomber pilot but a chief of state, as in 1914, the world might be plunged into war and several million people might die. But again, in a limited war using conventional weapons, the destruction is nowhere near total. Fifty years after the armistice, the war has lost its sharp outlines, new problems have plagued the world, and the race of man goes on.

When untold nuclear firepower is added to the equation, however, the outcome is different. In our preoccupation with jungle and paddy war in Vietnam, we have let this fact recede to the backs of our minds, but there is another—and all-encompassing—spectre of violence dominating our world. That spectre consists of arsenals of nuclear destruction designed to deter the very holocaust they render possible. To the brains and judgments of individual men has been coupled the power of the suns. Belligerents confront one another across the world—hostile, angry, fearful, threatening and being threatened—and the world is always on the brink of crisis. No longer does the nuclear warrior face his enemy man to man; now he is tangled in a vast complex of gadgets. He is expected to be a servomechanism to electronic devices, a brain plugged into a vast machine, a single circuit in an endlessly complex chain of command. He has been physically emasculated and intellectually extended. His is the brain, the decision unit; but the mechanical extensions of his senses and of his muscles embrace the globe.

Having now reported some behavioral-science research findings on human reactions to threat and crisis, and having sketched the changing nature of man's role in warfare, I should like to combine the two discussions. In doing so, I hope to show how these human reactions may confound the intent and functioning of these weapons systems. I will use just one example—

that of the nuclear submarine, usually considered the most reliable deterrence instrument in the American arsenal.

Forty-one of these Polaris submarines prowl the depths of the oceans, each carrying more explosive power than has been expended in the history of warfare. Each is linked to headquarters by radio waves. Each is commanded by officers chosen for their reliability. In 1964 some strategists began to question that reliability, suggesting that it might be safer if there were some kind of electronic lock-up of the missiles, a lock-up that could be released only by radio signal from headquarters—a Permissive Action Link, as it was designated. The Navy's response was an outraged assertion that these officers had been carefully selected, painstakingly trained, and continually tested, and that they could be totally trusted to behave responsibly— *never* to fire unless ordered to and *always* to fire if ordered to. And the admirals won the dispute. The PAL proposal was dropped and, following a large-scale rescreening program of the Strategic Air Command and Navy personnel who occupied key positions, the assumption was "bought" that the men were a totally reliable component in the decision system.

As we have seen, this very assumption may have been wrong. It may be wrong even with the safeguard of the most sophisticated selection and testing programs. Bruno Bettelheim, a psychiatrist who spent two years in Dachau and Buchenwald, reports of his fellow-prisoners that:

"The way a person acted in a showdown could not be deduced from his inner, hidden motives, which, likely as not, were conflicting. Neither his heroic nor his cowardly dreams, his free associations or conscious fantasies permitted correct predictions as to whether, in the next moment, he would risk his life to protect the life of others, or out of panic betray many in a vain effort to gain some advantage for himself."

The same is true of military officers. Roy Grinker and John Spiegel, psychiatrists who conducted studies of aircraft combat crews during World War II, reported the results of interviews, as well as the results of their intensive testing program. They concluded:

". . . no matter how 'normal' or 'strong' an individual is, he may develop a neurosis if crucial stress impinging on him is sufficiently severe. . . . Furthermore, it has been learned that the important psychological predispositions to 'operational fatigue' are usually latent and therefore difficult to detect until they are uncovered by catastrophic events. It must be concluded that for the vast majority the *only test for endurance of combat is combat itself.*"

They go on to state that military-security regulations prohibit their giving statistics as to how often soldiers collapse during combat!

Surely, you might say, the skills of selection boards and psychiatric procedures have been improved in the more than 20 years since the end of World War II. But not according to two of the men responsible for the Navy's selection and testing program. Captain R.L. Christy and Commander J.E. Rasmussen write that:

". . . the information which is available suggests that the present-day program is not nearly as effective as it was during World War II. . . . Moreover, the general training and experience level of psychiatrists and clinical psychologists assigned to these activities has generally decreased since the end of the Korean War."

They point out that "the program is least effective with high-level personnel where the examiner is faced with complex personality structures and sophisticated defense mechanisms," and conclude that:

"In simplest terms, it is unrealistic to expect any examiner to identify a reasonably well integrated individual's Achilles' heel and the unique combination of emotional and situational factors which could render him ineffective in the unforeseeable future."

What are the implications of this for nuclear weapons systems and their control personnel? The authors state that:

"When the manpower supply is plentiful, it well may be wise to adopt rather high and rigid psychiatric assessment standards for use with men assigned to nuclear weapons. *Some adjustment of the standards becomes necessary during periods of critical manpower shortage.*" (Emphasis added.)

And finally:

"Isolated instances exist, such as those recently reported in the press releases on the human-reliability problem, where obviously unfit individuals have been assigned to nuclear-weapons systems and subsequently have been responsible for potentially disastrous situations. There is no question that the majority of these individuals would have been disqualified for such an assignment if they had undergone psychiatric assessment prior to assuming their duties in a nuclear-weapons system. However, it has been the authors' experience that *the most potentially dangerous situations in the Navy have involved personnel who demonstrated no evidence of psychiatric disturbance at the time of their initial assignment to militarily sensitive duties.* Moreover, as a rule these individuals function in a highly effective fashion for a considerable length of time prior to developing psychiatric illness. Quite frequently, in retrospect, one could not have anticipated that the illness would have developed in this particular group of patients even though the presence of certain underlying psychopathology might have been recognized."

This, then, is the reality behind the military public-relations programs that would persuade us that we can "sleep tight tonight" since our fates are in the hands of infallibly reliable guardians. But behind the public facade, the military has also apparently recognized the frailty of man, for most weapons systems have been hedged with some sort of "fail-safe" arrangement. With the Polaris, for example, only after receiving a sequence of radio signals may a submarine commander fire his missiles at predetermined targets. And this firing requires that several men perform coordinated tasks. The captain and his crew are *never* supposed to decide on their own to fire those missiles. They *can*— it's technically possible—but they aren't supposed to. The captain must *coordinate* the efforts of a group of subordinates in order to fire the missiles, the assumption being that if the captain loses his judgmental ability, the others will retain theirs and thus prevent a mistaken firing.

Yet this assumption, too, is probably wrong. These are men who are chosen for compatibility, who have worked and thought and reasoned together. Chances are very good that they will react in the same way to any crisis. Grinker and Spiegel discuss the intense emotional bonds that grow among combat crews and the almost mystical sense of trust and interdependence that develops, concluding that "From a psychological point of view, the combat leader is a father and the men are his children." And even if the subordinates have doubts, there is research showing that they will most probably obey their captain's order. Paul Torrance has conducted research on B-26 crews and finds that when there is disagreement among them on a correct solution to a problem, the captain nearly always carries the others with him, regardless of whether his decision is "objectively" right or wrong. German officers obeyed, almost to the last man, even though many of them could not have truly accepted Hitler's doctrines. Laboratory subjects will obey an experimenter's instructions to the point of inflicting (so they think) intense electrical shocks on another subject, simply because an experimenter instructs them to do so "for the purposes of the research." When asked later why they did it, the subjects responded, with surprise at the question, "Why, we were told to." The drive to obey an authority seen as legitimate is almost overwhelming—even among students! How much stronger it must be for a military man not to behave mutinously when the "authority" is his senior officer.

My main point, however, is that these men control immense destructive power—and that they alone can check its use. Nothing but the sanity and cool judgment of *all* such key men in the world keep us alive today. Not only submarine commanders, but heads of state, secretaries of defense, radar observers, generals, and bomber-wing and missile-complex commanders must be able to think rationally, interpret information correctly, and act responsibly—keep cool heads in crisis after crisis, and wait patiently and soberly during times of calm. And it must be *all* of them.

This is the way the world is—poised on the brink of destruction because of the assumption that we can rely on the wisdom and cool judgment of these men at all times. Let me sketch a playlet demonstrating the possible consequences of our having failed to make an examination of that assumption before we acted on it.

Both the Soviet Union and the United States (not to mention France, Great Britain, China, and a dozen other countries that may soon join them) have long-range bombers, intercontinental missiles, shorter-range bombers and missiles, and fleets of submarines, all carrying arsenals of nuclear weapons and all under the control of men who must use their good judgment about striking or holding. Let's place our cast of actors on the submarines, since we started with them and since they are often touted as the most error-proof weapons system. If it's *conceivable* that an accident could occur with Polaris, leading to a decision that leads to an unintended war, then the danger is even greater with B-52s, Minuteman missile complexes, and short-range strike forces operating in the European corridors.

The United States and the Soviet Union also have been trying very hard to find ways of detecting these submarines so they cannot remain invulnerable in war. Suppose that in about 1970—in the midst of a Pueblo-like crisis—the Soviet Union responds by asserting that its own intelligence efforts are not inferior to those of the United States, that it has just perfected a radical new means of detecting submerged Polaris submarines. The United States, unwilling to believe this and afraid of domestic and allied reaction, denies that the Soviet Union has succeeded. The Soviet leaders, facing internal critics of the country's unaggressive stance over Vietnam, decide to demonstrate their military potency to the United States, the power of their technology to the world, and their vigorous leadership to their own people. They daringly plan to knock out one Polaris in such a way that everyone will be pretty certain that they did it, but no one could prove it. (Recall the Thresher incident if you like.) They track a submarine with one of their location ships (a fishing trawler); they find its range in the depths of the Indian ocean; they launch a salvo of long-range torpedoes. What they don't know is that the United States has made some recent sonic advances of its own. The submarine detects the oncoming torpedoes and takes evasive action, so it is not the "clean kill" upon which the attacker had relied, but a "near miss." The torpedoes explode, the submarine's hull is damaged, water begins to flood in, panic hits the crew. All is chaos. The men know they will die in a few minutes. The officers, on the basis of instrument readings, are certain that the Polaris has been hit by the Russians, but due to the damage, the depth at which they are cruising, and the attacker's jamming, they cannot establish radio contact with headquarters. Visions of mushroom clouds turning their families into ashes, visions that have haunted their minds for months, suddenly well to the surface; rage explodes in their bodies. Their hearts begin to pound, adrenaline shoots into their blood streams, their muscles expand, their breathing rates accelerate, their blood-sugar levels increase, their muscular strength nearly doubles—but . . . to what end? There is no charging foe, no soul-curdling yell to let out; there are only rows of cold buttons to push. Their reasoning falters, they can't think of alternatives, their memories function inadequately, they can't accurately process information coming in over their meters, they lose track of the long-term perspective and begin to act reflexively. The captain gives the command—"We must accomplish our mission. We will not die in vain." The crew, stunned and equally irrational, obeys.

The final act thus begins. The submarine is desperately trimmed for firing. The missiles lift from their capsules. Suddenly every decision level is in crisis, from radar observer to premier, and reflexes replace reflection. The Soviet Union, now under real attack, despairingly begins to retaliate; the United States orders its counterforce strike; the macabre dance of death unfolds, and in a few hours the world has been reduced to radioactive rubble. There are survivors, but the final curtain of dust does its work well; in a few generations the genetic key has been cruelly twisted, the race of man retreats into mutant extinction, the insects begin their rule of the next geological epoch.

This particular scenario is dramatic and unlikely. It is also tragic and possible. Five nations have thousands of separate weapons systems spread over the world, each with individual command units. As early as 1960, an authoritative report indicated that U.S. nuclear systems had already suffered 10 major accidents and about 50 minor ones—and this, of course, did not include the Thresher incident, the U-2 crashes, Vietnam activities, or nuclear bombs dropped off Spain and Greenland. Premier Khrushchev reportedly told Richard Nixon about an erratic Soviet missile that was destroyed by a signal from the ground as it headed toward Alaska, and on another occasion he implied that military commanders, on their own initiative, could order an attack on American U-2 bases. And these realities obtain in only a short period of time, and with the most "responsible" and sophisticated nuclear powers! In a few years there will be many more such nations. How much compounded will the chance of such crises be when Indonesia, Egypt, Israel, or South Africa have their own primitive nuclear complexes to reinforce their local quarrels? And we may be sure that the experience and technology of every other country will not match the expertise that provides the safeguards incorporated into a Polaris.

Coupling the individual human being to the power of the suns has meant that man's physiological response to crisis may no longer be functional—it may be a tragic flaw. He has become an unwitting victim of his own clever machinations. Now that we have attached our brains to intricate machines of near limitless power, and swaddled our tumescent bodies in frustrating physical inaction, even in the thick of warfare, man may become a self-destroying misfit.

This conceivable scenario with even the relatively foolproof Polaris highlights two basic assumptions on whose accuracy the fate of the world may rest: (1) that carefully selected men will retain cool judgment in an intense crisis, and (2) that even if one man fails, others will act as a "fail-safe" device. Yet, as I have demonstrated, *behavioral-science research shows that both assumptions are almost certainly false.*

We have been trapped, trapped by our egos, into believing that under any conditions we human beings can control both ourselves and the limitless machines to which we attach ourselves. This belief grew out of 17th-century rationalism, and has been reinforced by our spectacular success in mastering our environment.

And we *are* good—damned good—at creating a world in our image and in controlling that world. But there are little foxes, fragile seams, weak links, Achilles' heels, endemic to the human condition, and it well behooves us to lower our ego defenses enough to hear the voices of those who have examined human behavior at its extremes—the kind of extremes that can face decision-makers upon whose infallibility we rely. Sometimes these voices can tell us not only where we are making mistakes, but how we might rectify them.

In 1965 I suggested that the Polaris submarines retain their 1200-mile range missiles rather than getting 2500-mile range missiles; and that they be kept "off-station" or out of range of their targets by several hours' sailing time. This would mean that they *could* be used as retaliatory threats (which is what we claim they are for), but that they would *not* be in the provocative position of being able to strike first without warning, and that they could *not* cause a terrible escalation of the kind of incident I have just described. The responses from military and governmental personnel were that this was an intriguing idea, but since it would mean that Polaris could not be used in a "counterforce" role, the idea could not be taken seriously (as if the use of Polaris in counterforce targeting were somehow decreed by God, or as if counterforce strategies themselves had been proven desirable); or that it was "too late," since the long-range missiles were already in production; or that it would be pointless unless all of our weapons systems could receive the same treatment. In short, the reaction was one of unwillingness to cope with the really difficult problems, a response of fatalistic resignation to the uncontrollability of our destinies, and of detachment from the horror that we may be hastening.

National decision-makers must decide how to build weapons systems; they must decide whether to rely on "nuclear deterrence" or some other strategy. They must make endless assumptions (often unconsciously) about what people are like, how people will respond to crisis, to threat, to rage, to boredom, to too much or too little information, and so on and on. But it is not their business to read endless and often badly written research reports; it is beyond their scope to understand the complex scientific methods used in exposing the intricate dynamics of human behavior. Thus, these decision-makers often act in ignorance—they make false assumptions.

The scholar—the serious student of human behavior, like Robinson, Hermann, Holsti, Cannon, and myself—believes that someone must be responsible for examining policy in the light of the things we are learning about how human beings function. We believe we are failing in our mission unless we tap the policymaker on the shoulder and tell him we have reason to believe that he is making an unjustified assumption or an erroneous decision. And if he fails to respond to the tap, some of us believe we need to use whatever skills we can generate to collar and shake him, to shout in his ear—to *make* him listen. Otherwise, we are being irresponsible in our role as scholars.

What I have said in the last few pages is just one "minor" illustration of the kind of contribution we can make. Polaris *has* been improved over the years, on the basis of the designers' better understanding about the complexities of human behavior. It is far more difficult to devise a credible "accidental war" scenario now than it was in 1960—or 1965.

But many issues—from other, less stable weapons systems to negotiating strategies, from our policy towards China, or in Vietnam, to race relations or population growth—are crying for analysis and understanding. We behavioral scientists are not simply teaching industry how to administer personality tests better, or teaching the Defense Department how to design a bomber cockpit better, or teaching the Peace Corps how to train a volunteer better.

In many instances we are digging up information that is revolutionary—information that may suggest that a radical revision is necessary in the basic policy assumptions of our nation's decision-makers, and of decision-makers throughout the world.

January 1969

FURTHER READING SUGGESTED BY THE AUTHOR:

Arms Control for the Late Sixties by James E. Dougherty and J. F. Lehman, Jr. (Princeton, N.J.: Princeton University Press, 1967) is a study of current problems of arms control.

Sanity and Survival: Psychological Aspects of War and Peace by Jerome D. Frank (New York: Random House, 1968) applies psychological and other behavioral science findings to issues of deterrence and the control of nuclear weapons.

Nuclear Weapons, Missiles, and Nuclear War: Problems for the Sixties by Charles A. McClelland (San Francisco: Howard Chandler, 1960) presents a collection of studies on the problems and prospects of the nuclear age.

New Ways to Reduce Distrust Between the United States and Russia

MILTON ROSENBERG

"Nations are not people, and therefore the troubles between them cannot be understood through psychology." So runs a complaint that psychologists often hear from political scientists these days.

This point of view strikes me as both justified and unjustified, depending upon the kind of psychological approach being considered. Worthy of condescension is the sort of shallow psychologizing that suggests that national frustration leads directly to national aggression, or that attempts to explain particular wars as due to the madness of some specific historical figure or the basic personality structure of a whole people.

Another approach to the psychology of international relations, however, has been quietly maturing over the last decade. This approach assumes that the interests of various nations are frequently in real conflict—but that it is also common for international rivalries of the war-risking kind to be based largely upon attitudes that have no clear factual support. A guiding purpose in this new approach is to achieve a better understanding of the psychological forces that tend to drive both types of conflict toward limited, and then unlimited, war.

One important development is the attempt to focus some of the major theories of attitude change upon the relations between national élites. This may point ways out of dangerous international antagonisms that are rooted mainly in attitudes. And even where the clash of national interests is apparently "intractable," the alteration of background attitudes may still point ways out of the dilemma.

In this article, I hope to show how two of the major theories of attitude change might be applied in lowering some of the barriers to realistic settlement of international issues.

For simplicity I shall deal mainly with the interaction between the American and Soviet policy élites. But what is suggested here could be readily applied to aspects of the U.S.-Chinese or the Soviet-Chinese relationships—or, for that matter, to those of Israel and Egypt or any other set of national élites locked into mutual disdain and suspicion but not yet caught in long-term regression to active war, as we now are in Vietnam.

The *instrumental-learning* model of attitude dynamics was developed by Carl I. Hovland and Irving L. Janis and their associates, first in field experiments conducted for the Army during World War II and then at Yale. At its core is the idea that we learn to like or dislike (or to trust or distrust) someone or something by *reinforcement*—that is, because in the past the expression of our like or dislike has brought us rewards or reduced our needs.

The largest amount of experimental study has been devoted to two types of rewards. One is tied directly to what a person can gain if he changes some specific attitude—for instance, a person could reduce his anxiety over his health if he adopted an uncompromisingly negative attitude toward smoking. The second type of reward is due to increased social acceptance gained by moving one's attitudes toward the attitudinal standards set by others. Usually this happens not through mere cynical compliance, but through a gradual and "internalized" reorientation.

Changing the attitude of another person, according to this model, requires a series of steps:

—attract the attention of the person or groups whose attitudes you want to change;

—establish your credibility and trustworthiness;

—provide well-planned and informative communications that cast doubt upon the reasons and rewards that bolster the present attitude, and make change seem desirable by highlighting the rewards associated with the new, advocated attitude; and

—get the person or group to "rehearse" the new attitude for a while—to make its promised rewards seem more real and immediate.

Experimental work conducted by the Yale group and others has identified a number of factors that determine the success with which the various stages are negotiated. Among them are the basic credibility of the source of the persuasive communication; the way in which the communication is structured; the use of anxiety arousal; "role-playing" as a way of getting the person to consider the arguments and incentives that support the new attitude; the importance to the person of groups that support his attitude or its opposite; and personality factors making for general persuadability or rigidity.

Clearly, this model is relevant to changing the attitude pattern of distrust that continues to hamper movement toward true American-Soviet conciliation. The policy élites involved are composed of men playing roles that reduce flexibility. What limits these men most is that they feel *required* to distrust the opposing power and the assurances offered by its élite. Yet each side recognizes that the other's attitude of distrust must be converted toward trust if anything better than an easily-upset détente is to be achieved. Specifically, each side faces the problem of getting the other to believe its assurances that it will refrain from a surprise nuclear attack; that it will abide by arms-control and disarmament agreements (even when these cannot be effectively policed); that it will scrupulously adhere to sphere-of-influence agreements; and that it will accept necessary limitations of sovereignty as new and powerful international institutions are developed.

How are such attitudes of trust to be cultivated while policy élites still pursue and protect national interests? How can the Soviet-American "credibility gap" be closed?

The Yale experiments on credibility indicated that what seems to count most are the communicator's apparent status and expertise. But these have little bearing upon relations between policy-élite representatives, who are usually perceived by their opposite numbers as possessing both of these qualities in more than sufficient degree.

At this level there is, however, a more direct route

toward cultivating attitudes of trust. Though difficult to pursue, it must be taken, even while each nation strives to preserve and advance its own national interests. That route, to speak bluntly, is to stop posturing, faking, and lying.

Is it possible—even conceivable—that nations, in their relations with one another, can abandon the deceit that, since Machiavelli, has seemed essential to statecraft? Many specialists would immediately answer, in the tones of revealed doctrine, "As it was in the beginning, is now, and ever shall be, world without end. Amen." But at the risk of sounding naive, I believe that we need take a fresh look.

I suggest that the present international system is so inadequate and dangerous that the American and Soviet leaders have very compelling reasons to go beyond the limits of conventional *Realpolitik* and impose some moral order on their relationships. The exploration of this radical possibility could best begin with a direct assault upon the attitudinal problem of international distrust. There are probably many ways in which the behavioral sciences might help to mount such an assault. One would be the use of inter-nation gaming and simulation techniques—to provide "dry run" tests of an international system based upon a principle of generalized trust. Such studies might clarify just how feasible, how resistant to breakdown, a system of this sort would be, and how it might best be instituted.

But we need not wait. Immediate initiatives in honesty and self-revelation are now available for the seizing. Even though a great deal remains secret, even though the international system remains more closed than open, much could still be revealed to an antagonist under conditions that would allow him the opportunity for verification. There are possibilities in the direct revelation of data about arms technology, economic plans, the policy-formulation process itself. Such candor might well invite reciprocation. It might, in fact, set in motion expanding cycles of reciprocity that could eventually encompass most of the matters now surrounded by suspicion.

Another way of attempting to reduce attitudes of distrust would be, simply, to seek occasions that will require promises to be given—particularly promises that seem to incur some disadvantage for the promiser —and then to make sure that they are conscientiously fulfilled. This serves as almost incontrovertible evidence of reliability and credibility.

Additional useful suggestions can be drawn from the work of the Hovland group when we consider their emphasis (well backed by many experimental studies) upon appeals to the motives and incentives of individuals. How does this translate to the situation of one élite communicating with another? It highlights the importance of conducting diplomatic interaction so as to make clear to the other side the gains that are available if it will undertake an accommodating shift on some issue under negotiation.

This recommendation applies not so much to the general goal of reducing attitudes of distrust as to the conciliation of more specific issues. What if the United States offered the Soviet Union something it wanted in return for an arms quarantine of the Middle East? Or what if the Soviet Union offered us some equally meaningful reward for a U.S. guarantee that West Germany would not be allowed access to nuclear arms? In either instance the consequence might be conciliatory yielding. This would be due to changes of attitudes on the particular issues. But an exchange of such yieldings, particularly if accompanied by the recurring experience of promises kept, could alter the more basic attitudes of distrust that still persist between the American and Soviet policy-making groups.

Why, then, has this approach to conciliation rarely been used? One reason: Ingrained attitudes of mutual distrust inhibit easy exploration and flexible exchanges of conciliatory shifts. Another: The incentives occasionally offered to change attitudes are usually negative, not positive—threats and harassment, not attractive rewards. Leaders on either side may sometimes be forced to bow to such pressures, but their distrust and hostility will hardly diminish. Just the opposite: The élite group forced to yield, especially if humiliated, will await its opportunities for retribution.

The United States and Russia will continue to try to control each other's attitudes and actions by negative means as long as their leaders view their relationship as an extended zero-sum game—one side can win only if the other loses. Some issues, of course, are zero-sum; but many can be so structured that mutual gain *is* possible. Peace itself, after all, is a mutual gain.

Still, it is clear that possibilities for mutual gain cannot be found in each and every conflict. It would be better, therefore, to systematically rely on cross-trading. In other words, the advantage in one interest conflict is given to one side, while the advantage in another conflict is given to the other side. For example, the Soviet Union's refusal to allow unlimited inspection of its atomic facilities, and the United States' commitment to some form of nuclear force within NATO, are both seemingly unbudgeable stances. Might full, unscheduled inspections in the Soviet Union be traded for the permanent cancellation of plans for a NATO nuclear force?

The opportunities are vast. Both sides could continually review their priorities. How strongly do they desire particular concessions? What are they willing to offer in trade? Permanent trade-off negotiations could lead to large and thoroughgoing patterns of settlement.

After some initial success in trade-off negotiations, both groups would have experienced gains: The reduction of tensions, and domestic improvements made possible by shifting economic resources away from the defense sector. These gains would probably foster additional significant change in the attitudes of competitiveness and distrust that presently impede progress in American-Soviet conciliation. And this, in turn, would be likely to produce, on both sides, the strengthened conviction that trade-off negotiations are generally profitable even though they require abandonment of some earlier policy goals.

It would also be very useful if the United States and the Soviet Union were to immediately expand the search for shared problems that do *not* raise the apparent or fundamental issues of the lingering Cold War—problems in such comparatively manageable areas as technological development, scientific techniques, urban design, educational methods, crime control, and administrative organization. An institutionalized system that would foster greater East-West cooperation in the solution of such cross-national, domestic problems would probably be of clear benefit to both nations, as well as to the members of their respective blocs. And this, too, would further invalidate basic attitudes of competitiveness and distrust and foster further progress in resolving issues that have persisted in the framework of Cold War competition.

At least one other recommendation can be drawn from the instrumental-learning model of attitude change. Studies at Yale and elsewhere have shown that role-playing is a direct and effective method of changing attitudes. The subject becomes a kind of devil's advocate: He is required to argue for a viewpoint quite different from his own. In laboratory experiments, this often leads to attitude change—though exactly why and how this happens remains controversial.

In discussions between opposing groups of policy-makers, one would not expect or desire such facile shifts of attitude. But there is good reason to expect that role-playing techniques could help policy-makers of opposed groups to reexamine and, where necessary, revise the attitudes of suspicion and distrust they approach one another with. Further formal research on this process, and real-life experiments with it, would add considerably to the development of a technology of conciliation.

A word of warning is required. When a formerly hostile and untrusting opponent is beginning to change his attitudes, when he is letting his guard down, the temptation to take advantage of his new and tentative trust will often be great. Though short-run strategic and political gains may beckon in such a situation, they must be completely rejected—for nothing will so easily destroy the credibility of conciliatory communications and actions than a lapse into even a single unscheduled seizure of advantage.

The *consistency* theories represent a second major approach to attitude change, and they can add a good deal to our understanding of how to reduce distrust between policy élites. Though they differ in important ways, all these theories see an attitude as a combination of elements bound together in a kind of internal balance, so that any sizable disruption will bring into play a self-regulating dynamic that restores the original harmony. The basic assumptions, then, are that human beings need attitudinal consistency and are intolerant of inconsistency—and that when this consistency is disrupted, they often restore it through the process of attitude change.

So goes the general consistency-theory analysis. But to show its relevance to the problem of inter-élite distrust, we must get down to the particulars of one of the major theories of this type. The one that I will use is my own, though it reflects aspects of a related theory developed in cooperation with Robert Abelson. The fact that I use it here does not mean that it is superior to the other consistency models of attitude change, but simply that it is convenient for probing deeper into the problem of cross-élite attitude change.

Basic to this model is the definition of an attitude as a kind of psychological stance in which elements of *affect* and *cognition* are intimately related. The affective core of the attitude is simply the person's habitual feeling of like or dislike toward some "object," be that a person, an issue, a proposal, an institution, or an event. The cognitive component is simply his total set of beliefs about that liked or disliked object, particularly beliefs about how it is related to other things he is interested in and has feelings about.

To exemplify just what we mean by affective-cognitive consistency, and by the kind of inconsistency that fosters a change of attitude, we need to work through a concrete illustration. Let us take a hypothetical U.S. Senator standing on the periphery of the American decision-making circle just before the ratification of the atmospheric nuclear test-ban treaty. He approves of the treaty and plans to vote for it. This reflects his affective component—how he *feels* about the treaty.

In public debate he gives some of his reasons—the cognitive component: "The ban will slow the nuclear race. It will protect us from radioactive poisoning of the air. It will show the world that we mean it when we say we want peace." Privately, he adds other considerations: "It will probably freeze the nuclear race where it is now, while we still have a big advantage. Also, it should eventually open up some Eastern European markets we can use." Still another of his private reasons: "Judging by the latest polls, my stand should go over well with the liberal church and women's groups back home. Anyway, it should get the White House off my back and maybe get me better support from the National Committee in my next campaign."

If we check all of these reasons (technically, each is a cognition about the relationship between the attitude object and some other emotionally significant object), we find an interesting fact: The attitude object (the test-ban treaty) toward which the Senator has a positive feeling is, to him, positively related to such welcome developments as "opening up some Eastern European markets" and negatively related to such unwelcome possibilities as "radioactive poisoning of the air." This demonstrates a general principle: A positively-evaluated attitude object will typically be seen as bringing about desired goals or preventing undesirable ones; a negatively-evaluated object will be seen as blocking the way to desired goals, or fostering undesirable ones. Such affective-cognitive consistency has often been shown to be characteristic of stable attitudes. Furthermore, research has shown that the stronger and more extreme the basic positive or negative feeling toward the attitude object, the greater will be the person's certainty about the supporting beliefs.

How then, according to this model, can attitudes be changed? One must begin by trying to break up the internal harmony of beliefs and feelings—by inducing, or increasing, inconsistency. Most often, this is attempted by presenting arguments, data, and "facts" from sources that are seen as authoritative because of their prestige or expertise. The purpose is either to undermine beliefs that support the affective core of the attitude ("Experts say we can't be sure of our test-detection system, so how can we know the Russians won't keep testing and get far ahead of us?"), or to introduce new assertions that cast a different light—and thus induce contrasting feelings—on the subject ("If we stop testing, we simply cannot develop a good low yield, antimissile missile").

Introduce enough inconsistency and the subject will no longer be able to tolerate it. How much internal inconsistency a person can stand varies from attitude to attitude, situation to situation, and person to person. But everyone must reach a point where the piling up of inconsistency forces him to try to do something about it.

When a person's internal inconsistency becomes unbearable, one of three things will usually happen:
- He will simply retreat from the conflict. He will try to find some way to disregard the whole area of inconsistency.
- He will reject and expel the new cognitions that

are upsetting the old balance, and restore the initial attitude. (Incidentally, we may assume that this is what our hypothetical Senator did, since it is just what many real Senators did. The arguments *against* the nuclear test-ban treaty were simply not so telling and credible, or so important in the values they referred to, as were the arguments in favor of the treaty. In this case, the easiest route to reducing internal inconsistency was, ultimately, to reject the arguments that had generated it.)

■ He will yield to the new inconsistency-arousing cognitions, and—by changing his feelings about the attitude object—restore consistency.

This last is, of course, what is usually meant by attitude change.

Consistency theory also predicts, and has experimentally demonstrated, that the reverse form of attitude change is possible: *Feelings* can be altered first, and cognitions will follow. But, in real life, affect change resulting from prior cognition change is far more common.

What determines whether internal inconsistency brings about an overall change of attitude? First, the nature of the attitude itself. An attitude will probably be more easily changed by inconsistency if:

■ The number of beliefs that support the attitude is small.

■ The attitude object is believed to serve comparatively unimportant goals.

■ The person already holds a few beliefs that are inconsistent with his overall attitude.

■ The original attitude is isolated from most of the other attitudes of the individual—is itself, therefore, in a sense an inconsistency. (An example with a real Senator: Everett M. Dirksen's support of an earlier civil-rights bill was on the periphery of his essentially conservative concerns; his stance on civil rights has since undergone several sea changes.)

A second factor determining whether inconsistency leads to attitude change is how important the attitude is to a person's needs and essential motivations. The less the holding of the attitude serves to meet his real needs, the more easily—if threatened by inconsistency —it can be changed. Similarly, his attitudes are more easily altered when he does not need them for the roles he plays, or for maintaining good standing in the groups he identifies with.

From the foregoing, it is apparent why changing the attitudes of national leaders has been so difficult during the Cold War—even though both sides wanted to find some way out. The core attitudes of distrust, hostility, and competition have been so thoroughly anchored and buttressed by supporting beliefs, so strongly influenced by what leaders think their positions and "roles" require of them, that there has been very little room for flexibility.

This does not mean that evidence of good will or pacific intentions has been totally useless. But what usually happens is that these gestures are reinterpreted in ways that reduce their power to generate inconsistency and thus their power to affect attitudes. For example, an American offer of wheat sales would typically be interpreted by the Russians as a tactic to help the U.S. economy. And American leaders are likely to interpret Soviet offers to share information about industrial nuclear technology as a ploy to save the costs of research—rather than really to further general cooperation. Many leaders traditionally interpret gestures for peace as a mask for hostile intent—and bellicose gestures as proof of it.

Perhaps, therefore, the greatest positive good that came from the few very dangerous confrontations between the United States and the Soviet Union—particularly the Cuban missile crisis—has been that they gave the leaders of both nations some appreciation of how deeply each wanted to avoid stumbling into nuclear war. Since then, a number of steps toward avoiding danger have been taken, and they have probably thrown some inconsistency into the attitudes of mutual distrust. As a result, there is probably a fair opportunity today for each side to act in ways that could ultimately bring about changed attitudes. How can this best be done? The consistency approach offers some leads.

One clear recommendation is that, before the competing policy groups undertake to revise each other's attitudes, they study what these attitudes really are, and what beliefs are built into them. Too often policy-makers seem confused about the perceptions and purposes that lie behind the policy positions taken by the competing power. "Riddles wrapped in mysteries inside enigmas" lie more often in the eye of the observer than the observed. Surely, within the great mass of white papers, diplomatic conversations, propaganda releases, and policy rationalizations that flow from Washington or Moscow there should be enough material for an educated reconstruction of how opposing leaders really think and feel about an issue, and how they structure policy around it. Close study of this sort would help isolate the issues on which the other side would be comparatively receptive to actions and messages that could generate internal inconsistency.

Obviously these issues, at the present time, would

be on the outer edge of major policy and have little immediate effect on important conflicts. But the real purpose of such early efforts is to lower the opposing side's defense against information and action that might create inconsistency in more central attitudes. If either side could convince the other that it really *does* favor cultural exchange in order to reduce tension, rather than to make propaganda—or that it really *wants* disengagement in Central Europe to avoid military confrontations, rather than to gain some devious advantage—then the day will be much closer when the very center of the web of distrust and competition can be directly assaulted.

But can such direct assault succeed when the core issues still seem virtually irreconcilable? How is this to be done? This is where the consistency approach is especially pertinent. It suggests strongly that *there are no truly intractable, unchangeable attitudes*. Instead, there are less resistant and more resistant ones. Where resistance is high, this is because the affective portion of the attitude is supported by a large number of detailed beliefs that are consistent with it—and also because the attitude itself is consistent with the role demands and ideologies that leaders must live up to. For such an attitude to be changed it must be bombarded with a continuing, unrelenting stream of inconsistency-generating communications and events— and the more peripheral attitudes to which it is tied must also be exposed to pressures for change.

To reverse the attitudes of distrust with which the Soviet and American élites approach and misinterpret each other, either or each of them must undertake an unflagging display of trustworthiness—and give strong, unequivocal evidence that its paramount desire is conciliation. In this light Charles Osgood's GRIT strategy is very relevant. Osgood recommends a long series of unilateral, tension-reducing initiatives on the part of the United States, even if no sign of reciprocation appears from the Soviets for some time. He also maintains that concrete actions speak much louder—and less ambiguously—than words.

For too long both the United States and the Soviet Union have been lagging in this regard. On the American side, occasional actions in the Kennedy years and in the last period of the Eisenhower era may have worked, whether by intention or not, to generate some inconsistencies in Soviet core attitudes of distrust. But these actions were never designed as part of a strong, well-focused plan for reducing tension. Today the situation is worse. What probably stands out most to the Soviets is our past escalation of the Veitnam war and our continuing rejection of those opportunities for realistic settlement that are apparently available.

Still other recommendations can be drawn from the consistency approach, particularly from the variants developed by other authors. Here is one example out of a number of possibilities: Both Fritz Heider and Theodore Newcomb have studied the kind of consistency that is found *between* rather than *within* the attitudes of separate people. And both have reported considerable supporting evidence for this proposition: People who are tied together by friendship or more formal role relationships tend toward mutual consistency on important attitude issues. Nevertheless, they will sometimes encounter inconsistency between their separate attitudes. When this happens, the formally or emotionally subordinate person will usually alter his attitude to bring it into consistency with that of the other person.

This proposition is not surprising, but put this way it does have considerable practical value. What it suggests is that attempts to produce attitude change through arousing inconsistency will work best if we first learn as much as possible about members of the "target group" and their relationships with one another. Who are the key men, why, and what are they like?

The most influential, in governmental as in business élites, are not always the most visible. When we know who the crucially placed people in the opposing élite are—and, particularly, when their importance is based upon their analytic or strategic skills—we have found the people toward whom our initial attempts at inconsistency arousal ought to be especially directed. If *their* attitudes begin to shift, the effect may spread across the élite group more rapidly than could otherwise happen.

In all that I have said up to now I have been urging greater adventurousness in the attempt to reduce inter-élite distrust. But, of course, real-life constraints and responsibilities often inhibit the taste for adventure and innovation. The policy-élite groups of the contesting powers are still limited by their attitudes of distrust toward one another, and by concerns over the domestic political consequences of a too rapid or dramatic movement toward international conciliation. Also they are sometimes hampered by the "prudential" (the word is borrowed from certain strategic analysts) definition of their roles—that is, they sometimes take it as their obligation to imagine the worst they can about the opposing power's motives and intentions and then to act on the assumption that what they have imagined is accurate.

Thus most of the suggestions made here would probably not be acceptable to typical members of the policy élites of the contesting powers. However, desperation over the impasse imposed by the Cold War, and fear of escalation, have moved some leaders to re-examine their own attitudes about the plans and intentions of their opposite numbers. This development had, in fact, progressed quite far—until it began to languish and lose relevance in the wake of the Vietnam war.

If the Vietnam war should end with a setback for those American policy-makers still committed to the John Foster Dulles "roll-back of Communism" and "brinksmanship" doctrines, we may see an energetic renewal of the search for meaningful conciliation. Awareness of the possibilities discussed here could make that search much more productive. And in the meantime it can foster preparation for new peace initiatives and help to keep alive the prospect of ultimate conciliation.

April 1968

FURTHER READING SUGGESTED BY THE AUTHOR:

Communication and Persuasion by Carl I. Hovland and Irving L. Janis (New Haven, Conn.: Yale University Press, 1953).

An Alternative to War or Surrender by Charles Osgood (Urbana, Ill.: University of Illinois Press, 1963).

Attitude Organization and Change by Milton J. Rosenberg, Carl I. Hovland, *et al.* (New Haven, Conn.: Yale University Press, 1960).

International Behavior: A Social-Psychological Analysis edited by Herbert C. Kelman (New York: Holt, Rinehart & Winston, 1965). See "Images in Relation to the Policy Process—American Public Opinion on Cold-War Issues" by Milton J. Rosenberg.

ABM and the Arms Race

MARVIN KALKSTEIN

In recent months there has been extensive discussion and debate of the ABM issue, and it has been generally recognized as one of the key issues presently facing the nation. On Friday, March 14, 1969, President Nixon announced the administration's decision with regard to ABM. Now it remains for Congress and the public to determine where we go from here.

With the Presidents' announcement, we now have a set of specific recommendations and arguments upon which to focus our attention. The President suggested that the proposed deployment is designed to fulfill three objectives:

1) protection of our land-based retaliatory forces against direct attack by the Soviet Union

2) defense of the American people against the kind of nuclear attack that Communist China is likely to be able to mount within the decade

125

3) protection against the possibility of accidental attack from any source

Let us first look at the question of protecting our land-based retaliatory forces. The President has said that "the imperative that our nuclear deterrent remains secure beyond any possible doubt requires that the United States must take steps now to insure that our strategic retaliatory forces will not become vulnerable to Soviet attack." It should be recognized that our present deterrent is comprised of a mix of nuclear-weapons systems including, according to Defense Department figures as of September 1968, 1,054 land-based intercontinental ballistic missiles, 656 sea-based Polaris missiles on 41 nuclear-powered submarines, and 646 strategic air bombers. This force then consists of 1,710 ballistic missiles and 646 bombers capable of delivering a total of 4,200 nuclear weapons against an enemy. The same source indicates that the Soviet Union possesses 900 land-based ICBMs, 45 sea-based ballistic missiles, and 150 strategic air bombers capable of carrying a total of about 1,200 nuclear warheads. According to Defense Department estimates, even as few as 200 delivered warheads could cause 50 million Soviet fatalities and destroy 70 percent of their industry. Thus, it should be obvious that present Soviet forces do not pose a credible threat to our retaliatory forces. Concern for the security of our retaliatory forces seems to stem from the fact that the Soviet Union reached its present level of ICBMs through a large buildup in the past two or three years.

The main argument supporting this contention that the Soviet Union is striving to achieve a first-strike capability has been the recent disclosure by Secretary of Defense Melvin Laird of intelligence information regarding the Soviet deployment of the SS-9 missile, thought to be capable of carrying nuclear warheads with a yield as large as

20 or 25 megatons. Other estimates put the size of the warhead at five-ten megatons. Since the main advantage in using high-yield warheads would be to attack hardened missile sites rather than cities, Laird has cited their deployment as evidence of Soviet first-strike intentions. However, the number of SS-9 missiles currently deployed is given as 200 and on the basis of the recent rate of deployment, it is predicted that the number will reach 500 in 1975.

Neither of these numbers represents a credible first-strike potential; indeed, what is truly incredible is the suggestion that the United States deterrent force is suddenly to become wholly inadequate. Even equipping the SS-9 with Multiple Independently Targetable Re-entry Vehicles (MIRVs) will not change this picture, as I will discuss later. Furthermore, former Secretary of Defense Clark Clifford was aware of the same intelligence at the time of his January 15, 1969, defense-posture statement, and he was neither unduly alarmed nor as prone to predict so many Soviet SS-9 weapons in 1975. He felt that their deployment would probably soon level off. The recent build-up, he stated, was most likely motivated more from a desire to achieve parity with United States forces rather than an attempt to arrive at a first-strike capability against our forces.

Apart from the SS-9, there appears to be further concern in the Administration based upon the Soviet's having achieved a capability of producing a sizeable number of submarines equipped with ballistic missiles. At the indicated rate of seven submarines a year, however, it will be many years before this force equals ours. They may be regarded as a threat to our land-based bombers, since they might afford a shorter warning time. But the Perimeter Acquisition Radar (PAR) would be to some extent helpful as a means of affording early warning.

Another factor cited by the President in the buildup of Soviet strategic forces is their development of the Fractional Orbital Bombardment System (FOBS). FOBS are recognized as having very low accuracy and therefore cannot properly be regarded as a threat to our hardened land-based missiles. They may, however, represent a threat to our bomber forces. By using a low orbit, it is possible that they could reduce the warning time that we would have from our Ballistic Missile Early Warning System (BMEWS), thus making it more difficult to get our aircraft airborne before their bases are struck. However, according to former Secretary Clifford, it would not reduce the possibility of early detection by our planned Over-the-Horizon (OTH) and satellite-borne missile warning systems. He suggested as an additional available option that we can increase from 40 to 60 percent the proportion of bombers held on 15-minute ground alert, assuring us of the survival of at least 385 planes capable of delivering more than 10,000 megatons of nuclear explosives.

Probably the most secure component of our retaliatory force is the Polaris submarine fleet. Secretary Laird in his testimony before the Senate Armed Services Committee and the Disarmament Subcommittee of the Foreign Relations Committee on March 20 and 21, 1969, intimated that this security may be threatened by the mid-1970's. However, in no way did he substantiate this possibility. The nation's leading technical experts for years have regarded the Polaris submarine as invulnerable and none as yet have indicated any change in this opinion. The most recent public information is that detection and tracking of these submarines at any substantial distance is still beyond the realm of present technical capability and is likely to remain so for a considerable time into the future. It is obvious that unforeseen developments might negate any weapons system we might have, including an ABM system, but such consideration cannot be used as a major basis for defense policy. At least, not if we wish to pursue sound policies.

In discussing our capability against "Greater-Than-Expected Threats," former Secretary Clifford regarded only an extensive, effective Soviet ABM defense as a counter to our submarine-launched missiles. Apparently, he was not as impressed as Secretary Laird with potential Soviet threats to our Polaris submarines. Of our additional available options, one of which allows the expansion of Sentinel to include defense of our Minutemen sites, he stated that, "We need not take any of these steps until we have some evidence that the threat is actually beginning to emerge." Obviously, his assessment of our intelligence information was quite different from Laird's. Or, quite possibly, Secretary Laird's position is based on reasons he has been unwilling to discuss. Clifford concluded that "taking our strategic posture as a whole, we have an ample margin of safety and we can afford to proceed with due deliberation on very costly new programs."

In ruling out increasing the number of sea- and land-based missiles and bombers as a means to insure the survival of our retaliatory forces, the President argued that such a course provides only marginal improvement of our deterrent. This seems indeed to be true but can only be regarded as such by recognizing the fact that our present forces represent an overwhelmingly large deterrent. Quite rightly, with such an overwhelming deterrent, any increase at this time would be of marginal value.

A second option rejected by the President would be to further harden our ballistic missile forces by putting them in more strongly reinforced underground silos. Harold Brown, former Secretary of the Air Force, has described new harder silos as "a form of ABM defense." Increasing the hardness by about a factor of 10 would reduce the probability of one SS-9 destroying a Minuteman missile by from 90 percent to about 20 percent. To regain a 90 percent destruction capability, the Soviet Union would need 10 times as many such weapons as would presently be the case. Converting their SS-9 missiles to MIRVS would not appreciably affect the situation. The probability of destroying a Minuteman with three five-megaton warheads is not much greater than with one 25-megaton warhead. The introduction of superhard silos would, in fact, have a number of advantages for protecting our ICBMs. Since concrete is a main ingredient, it would be much cheaper and far more reliable. I have a high expectation that concrete would do what it is expected to do, whereas the highly complex ABM system could fail for a variety of reasons. Finally, such an approach would not give rise to a new round in the arms race. At the very least, moving to superhard silos should allow us to delay an ABM deployment for a number of years.

Finally, the economics of attempting to provide an effective defense of our land-based missiles should not be overlooked. The present proposed figures for the Safeguard system will allow the deployment of only a relatively small number of Spartan and Sprint missiles at each site. (The Spartan has a 400-mile to 500-mile range and can afford defense coverage to a very large area; the Sprint is a 25-mile to 30-mile range missile that can provide protection against an incoming missile around the terminal point.) The first two ABM sites to be deployed by 1973 are planned to protect our Malmstrom, Montana, and Grand Forks, North Dakota, Minuteman bases, each of which have about 150 Minuteman missiles. On the basis of 700 Spartan missiles in the original Sentinel System, we can expect that 60 to 70 Spartans will be allotted per ABM base. The increased cost for the Safeguard system suggests that a similar number of Sprints may be assigned to each base. The reason for rejecting the Sentinel defense of our cities against Soviet attack is that area defense based only on Spartan will not work against a sophisticated and large attack of the sort that the Soviet Union can launch. Thus the protection of our missiles will depend upon the hardpoint defense provided by the Sprint missiles. Sixty to 70 Sprints can at best provide protection against an equal number of Soviet warheads. Obviously, in 1973 only a handful of our Minuteman missiles will be protected, and it won't be until several years later that the Safeguard system will encompass our full Minuteman force. Even then, its capability to cope with a Soviet first-strike will be questionable.

Should the Soviet Union contemplate a first-strike attack, they would have to use at least as many warheads as we have Minuteman missiles. With less than half as many Sprints as Minutemen, more than half our Minutemen would be virtually unprotected. To protect all our Minutemen (which admittedly may not be a necessary aim), we would need at least as many Sprints. If, as is likely, an attacker would assign more than one warhead per Minuteman to insure himself of a high probability of destroying our Minuteman, we would have to increase the number of Sprints accordingly. Furthermore, if we desire a high probability of destroying an incoming missile, we would have to assign several Sprints for each warhead in their force. Even if our objective is to assure ourselves of the survival of a few hundred Minuteman missiles after an enemy first-strike, the number of Sprints needed may range into the several thousands, requiring the expenditure of tens of billions of dollars for Sprints alone.

Greatly increased expenditures would undoubtedly be

required for the radar and computer components of the system if the system is even to suggest the survival of an adequate retaliatory force. At present, our Missile Site Radars are not sufficiently hardened to withstand the effects of a high-yield airburst. Several incoming warheads targeted on the MSR would stand a good chance of destroying or incapacitating it. Once this has occurred, all the remaining Sprints dependent upon that MSR will have become useless. To avoid this, in addition to greater hardening for the MSRs, considerable expenditures will be required for more MSRs. We would thus be talking about spending tens of billions of dollars just to make it possible that Safeguard has some chance of providing the protection that the President desires.

The President's second proposed objective for his ABM was to protect the American people from a nuclear attack by Communist China. The first line of defense against such an attack is prevention, and that is precisely what our deterrent forces are meant to accomplish. If our deterrent forces can be relied upon to prevent a nuclear attack by a large strategic force of the Soviet Union, they should be more than adequate against the virtually nonexistent strategic nuclear forces of Communist China. In spite of the militant talk by the Chinese and about them, former Secretary of Defense Robert S. McNamara in his September 18, 1967, speech announcing the previous Sentinel decision acknowledged that "China has been cautious to avoid any action that might end in a nuclear clash with the United States—however wild her words—and understandably so. We have the power not only to destroy completely her entire nuclear offensive forces but to devastate her society as well." Furthermore, should China be so "insane and suicidal" as to contemplate an attack upon the United States, there would be means available to her for which an ABM defense would be inadequate. There are many ways of overcoming such a defense. An ABM system would be ineffective against attack by means other than ICBMs—for example, low-flying aircraft, cruise missiles, missiles launched from offshore submarines, and missiles smuggled into ports from other locations and then detonated. In addition, there are a number of easy and inexpensive means by which an ICBM can penetrate an area defense such as the proposed system would provide for our cities. These penetration aids include fragmentation of the missile's booster rocket, chaff, decoys, electronic jamming, and radar blackout produced by the predetonation at high altitude of an incoming missile. All of these are relatively simple and at least some would be likely to be incorporated by an enemy whose initial ICBM deployment would be faced with an ABM. It would be naive to assume that a nation capable of the effort to produce an ICBM system would not add some such minor extra effort to its initial ICBM system if it is aware that it will be faced with an ABM system such as the proposed one.

The third stated objective was protection against the possibility of accidental attacks. An accidental attack is, by definition, an unintentional attack, and one might reasonably presume that a nation whose missile was accidentally fired would prefer to prevent its warhead from exploding upon an enemy target. A number of mechanical means are employed by the United States to reduce the likelihood of accidents, and it is reasonable to expect that safety measures are employed by other nations as well. Since the prevention of accidental attack is in the mutual interest of all nations involved, in exchange of the independent safety features employed by each nation should be possible, perhaps leading to a weapons-safety conference of the nuclear-weapon nations. An obvious additional desired feature would be to have provisions for the destruction or disarming of an accidentally fired missile by the nation to whom it belongs before such missile could reach its target. Senator Stuart Symington at the hearings before the disarmament subcommittee of the Senate Foreign Relations Committee suggested that we already can do this with our missiles. At the time of these hearings, both Secretary Laird and his deputy, David Packard, concurred in the view, but the Pentagon has since asked that their public testimony be changed to deny the possibility of disarming the missiles once fired. The difficulty with a destruct capability may be that one cannot prevent the nation under attack from triggering such a mechanism and so, for the purposes of having an assured deterrent, this destruct capability could present problems. Although I am generally not inclined to suggest purely technological solutions, it would seem that a tamper-proof destruct mechanism should be in the realm of technical feasibility. Along these lines, a suggestion to prevent unintentional or irrational firing of the Polaris submarine weapons could also safeguard against accidental firings as well. In 1964, a Permissive Action Link was suggested that would have provided a kind of electronic lock-up of the missiles, a lock-up that could be released only by radio signal from headquarters. This proposal was evidently dropped but might well be worth renewed consideration.

It is encouraging to note from the remarks in his announcement that the President is aware of some of the problems and dilemmas of the present arms balance. He noted that "there is no way that we can adequately defend our cities without a loss of life," stating in his announcement, "the heaviest defense system we consider, one designed to protect our major cities, still could not prevent a catastrophic level of United States fatalities from a deliberate all-out Soviet attack." At his press conference, he concluded that the only way we can save lives is to prevent war.

A significant point in the President's announcement was his continued emphasis on his desire to avoid programs that might be regarded as provocative to the Soviet Union. Under the present system of deterrence, this is a crucial point and one that we must not lose sight of. For most of the 1960's, we and the Soviet Union have maintained a strategic weapons relationship that can be characterized as one of stable deterrence. Under this relationship, both sides are assured that a nuclear attack by one side will be returned by a second-strike attack causing unacceptable damage to the initial attacker. This is so because both sides have sufficiently large and secure forces that even after being hit by a first-strike, significant residual retaliatory forces will remain. The recognition of this condition and the experience gained in living for several years under this condition have contributed to the stability of United States-Soviet Union military relations and to the relaxation of strategic tensions between the two superpowers. Anything that might threaten to alter this condition would be destablizing and a cause for increased tension. It is for this reason that provocative acts are to be avoided. This is as true for the Soviet Union as it is for the United States and should be as well-recognized by their leaders as it seems to be by ours. We would be doing ourselves as well as the Soviet Union a disservice to act on the supposition that they are being so foolhardy as to pursue a first-strike capability.

The proposed Safeguard system, whether regarded as provocative or not in its present form, leaves the door open to more provocative ABM steps on our part in the future. Unfortunately, the proposed "thin" ABM system with the annual review and evaluations suggested by the President can still be regarded as most likely a first step toward the construction of a thick system. What has happened in the past two months is that the Army was caught trying to take a giant step toward the thick system and has had to settle for presidential permission to take a small step instead.

In addition, there are other critical weapons decisions facing the President now. The most destabilizing strategic-weapons development in recent years has been the development of the Multiple Independently Targetable Re-entry Vehicle (MIRV), which will be ready for deployment within a few years. The deployment of MIRV in the absence of an extensive ABM on the other side would raise the specter of first-strike intentions. It is the ability to destroy with one of your missiles more than one of an opponent's missiles that puts a premium on striking first and hence is destabilizing. If the President sincerely wishes to avoid extreme provocation, he should make the decision now to refrain from testing, procurement, and deployment of MIRV. Continuing with MIRV cannot help but provoke the Soviet Union to expand both its offensive and defensive forces.

The President has put considerable emphasis in his announcement on prospective arms-limitation talks with the Soviet Union. If we are to move to an era of negotiation, as has been the President's pledge, it should be more fruitful if we do not use the tactics of confrontation as a bargaining ploy. If both sides are truly interested in halting the arms race, as seems to be the case, meaningful negotiations should proceed without introducing extraneous complicating factors, such as the Safeguard ABM Program. If we are to avoid proceeding beyond a point of no (or difficult) return, we must begin *now* to seek agreements. It is recognized that negotiations, of necessity, tend to be difficult and complex. However, once MIRV is fully developed and ready to deploy, the problems of controlling a strategic arms-limitation agreement become more severe. Therefore, it would be highly desirable to seek an *immediate* joint moratorium on the procurement and deployment of new strategic-weapons systems. This would include ABM, MIRV, and similar bomber systems. The moratorium should also include range testing of new missile systems, so as to stop MIRV before it is too late. Such a moratorium would afford the time and the atmosphere for achieving a more comprehensive agreement.

In the final analysis, the only permanent solution to the ABM and MIRV questions is a negotiated agreement limiting both defensive and offensive weapons systems. This must become the President's and the country's prime objective.

I would like now to discuss the areas of public concern and the ways in which ABM has become a public issue. The shifts of the Defense Department in their attempts to sell the nation on ABM has brought into serious question their credibility, which already had been brought into doubt as a result of the Vietnam war. The obvious reason for the Army's attempt to locate Sentinel sites near cities, when, under the concept of a thin area defense, the sites could have just as well been located several hundred miles from the cities, was that it would afford them an easier opportunity to proceed to a thick system, which appears to be their ultimate objective. The one-month period of review of the ABM question appears to have been used mainly as an attempt to cool public concern and outrage and to seek means by which a modified system could be made more palatable to the American public and Congress.

The shifting arguments and somewhat conflicting testimony of Secretaries Laird, Packard, and Rogers have done little to restore confidence in the administration's handling of this vital defense issue. The annual review of the ABM that the President proposes assures the proponents of an expanded ABM system ample opportunity to push their case on a regular and continuing basis. The history with regard to the ABM has shown that appropriate intelligence to support the Army position can be found or manufactured almost on demand. Thus, intelligence that the Soviet is continuing to increase their numbers of offensive weapons deployed will be the basis for demands to extend the number of ABMs protecting our land-based missiles, and any intelligence, regardless of how little substance, suggesting sophistication in the developing Chinese ICBMs will be used as strong arguments for expanding to a thick system around many of our cities. It is hard to imagine that the President would be able to withstand such future pressures since, in deciding to support an ABM system, he found it expedient to yield to military pressures even when there were strong Congressional and public forces operating in the opposite direction. It remains for the public to question and to apply pressure in order to contain Pentagon interests.

A second and perhaps most obvious reason for public interest is the huge amounts of money involved. At a time when our cities are deteriorating, people are going hungry, and our educational system is near collapse, tens of billions of dollars are spent on military systems without question of value or need. The threat to our country is not from foreign missiles but from a breakdown of our society from within. If there is to be a re-ordering of our national priorities, the public must take a hand. The ultimate aspect of public concern should be the arms race. The ABM issue may represent a final breakthrough in public awareness that the arms race must be a vital concern for everyone. It is hard to believe that we have lived with the threat of nuclear annihilation for more than 20 years and only now does the public seem to be aware and concerned about it. Previous issues of arms policy were never viewed in relation to the arms race but rather in terms of personal concerns with regard to fallout in the case of nuclear test-ban considerations and personal responses to the fallout-shelter program. For the first time, the arms race itself has become a matter of public concern and will have to remain so until it is ended or de-escalated.

I would like to conclude by discussing briefly the public role on these issues. If we consider the decision-making process in this country, we find that on defense issues the decision making takes place at a corporation level or above. Basically, a few large industrial concerns, the Pentagon, members of Congress, and the administration are involved and the public takes no or little part in such decisions. If there is a re-ordering of national priorities, the issues that would become important would include housing, welfare, education, and transportation. These are "people" issues and "people" would have to be involved in the decisions relating to them. However, unless we get this re-ordering of priorities, there will be little opportunity to address ourselves to these issues. It is, therefore, necessary that defense be made a "people" issue too. This suggests a positive action-oriented role for the public at large.

June 1969

FURTHER READING SUGGESTED BY THE AUTHOR:

ABM: Yes or No? by Donald Brennan, William O. Douglas, Leon Johnson, George S. McGovern, Jerome Wiesner, with an introduction by Hubert H. Humphrey (Santa Barbara, Calif.; Center for the Study of Democratic Institutions, 1969).

American Scientists and Nuclear Weapons Policy by Robert Gilpin (Princeton, N.J.: Princeton University Press, 1965).

Debate the Antiballistic Missile edited by Eugene Rabinowitch and Ruth Adams (Chicago: Bulletin of the Atomic Scientists, 1967).

The Price of War

BRUCE M. RUSSETT

"Peace" stocks are up; "war" stocks are down; congressmen scrutinize Pentagon expenditures with newly jaundiced eyes. Any (New Left) schoolboy can rattle off a list of the top ten defense contractors: General Electric, Boeing, General Dynamics, North American Aviation. . . . Scholars and journalists have worked hard lately, and now almost everyone knows who *profits* from defense spending. But who knows who *pays* for it?

Nothing comes free, and national defense is no exception. Yet curiously little attention has been paid to the question of which segments of American society and its economy are disproportionately sacrificed when defense spending rises. Despite some popular opinion to the contrary, our economy is a good deal less than infinitely expansible. Something has to give when military expenditures take larger bites out of the pie. But when this happens, what kinds of public and private expenditures are curtailed or fail to grow at previously established rates? What particular interests or pressure groups show up as relatively strong or relatively weak in maintaining their accustomed standards of living? And which of them are better able to seize the opportunities offered when international conflict cools off for awhile?

The questions, of course, are implicitly political, and they are important. But the answers have to be sought within economic data. What we want, in a sense, is a "cost-benefit" analysis of war or the preparations for war, an analysis that will tell us not only who most profits from war, but who most bears its burden. Apart from the direct costs in taxation and changes in wages and prices, which I will not go into here, there are the equally significant costs in social benefits, in opportunities foregone or opportunities postponed.

What I want to do here is to examine *expenditures*—by categories of the gross national product (GNP), by their function and by governmental unit—to see what kinds of alternative spending suffer under the impact of heavy military spending. The necessary data are available for the period 1939-1968, and they allow us to see the effects of two earlier wars (World War II and the Korean War) as well as the burdens of the current Vietnam venture.

First, however, an overview of the changing level of defense expenditures may be helpful. For 1939, in what was in many ways the last peacetime year this nation experienced, defense expenditures were under $1.3 billion. With the coming of war they rose rapidly to a still unsurpassed peak of $87.4 billion in 1944. By contrast, the 1968 figure was around $78.4 billion, reflecting a build-up, for the Vietnam War, from levels of about $50 billion in the first half of this decade. The raw dollar figures, however, are deceptive because they reflect neither inflation nor the steady growth in the economy's productive capacity that makes a constant defense budget, even in price-adjusted dollars, a diminishing burden.

The graph shows the trend of military expenditures as a percentage of GNP over the past thirty years.

We immediately see the great burdens of World War II, followed by a drop to a floor considerably above that of the 1930s. The Cold War and particularly the Korean action produced another upsurge in the early 1950s to a level that, while substantial, was by no means the equal of that in the Second World War. This too trailed downward after the immediate emergency was past, though again it did not retreat to the previous floor. In fact, not since the beginning of the Cold War has the military accounted for noticeably less than 5 percent of this country's GNP; not since Korea has it had as little as 7 percent.

This repeated failure to shrink the military establishment back to its prewar level is a phenomenon of some interest to students of the dynamics of international arms races and/or Parkinson's Law. It shows up even more clearly in the data on military personnel, and goes back almost a century to demonstrate the virtual doubling of the armed forces after every war. From 1871 to 1898 the American armed forces numbered fewer than 50,000; after the Spanish-American War they never again dropped below 100,000. The aftermath of World War I saw a leveling off to about 250,000, but the World War II mobilization left 1,400,000 as the apparent permanent floor. Since the Korean War the United States military establishment has never numbered fewer than about 2,500,000 men. Should the post-Vietnam armed forces and/or defense portion of the GNP prove to be higher than in the early and mid-

1960s, that will represent another diversion from private or civil public resources and a major indirect but perhaps very real "cost" of the war.

Returning to the graph, we see the effect of the Vietnam build-up, moving from a recent low of 7.3 percent in 1965 to 9.2 percent in 1968. This last looks modest enough, and is, when compared to the effects of the nation's two previous major wars. At the same time, it also represents a real sacrifice by other portions of the economy. The 1968 GNP of the United States was well in excess of $800 billion; if we were to assume that the current war effort accounts for about 2 percent of that (roughly the difference between the 7.3 percent of 1965 and the 9.2 percent of 1968) the dollar amount is approximately $16 billion. That is, in fact, too low a figure, since some billions were already being devoted to the war in 1965, and direct estimates of the war's cost are typically about $25 to $30 billion per year. The amounts in question, representing scarce resources which might be put to alternative uses, are not trivial.

I assume that defense spending has to come at the expense of something else. In the formal sense of GNP proportions that is surely true, but it is usually true in a more interesting sense as well. Economics is said to be the study of the allocation of scarce resources; and, despite some periods of slack at the beginning of war-time periods (1940-1941 and 1950), resources have generally been truly scarce during America's wars. Major civilian expenditures have not only lost ground proportionately (as would nevertheless happen from a military spending program financed entirely out of slack) but they have also failed to grow at their accustomed rates, they have lost ground in constant dollars as a result of inflation, or they have even declined absolutely in current dollars. During World War

II, for example, such major categories as personal consumption of durable goods, all fixed investment, federal purchases of nonmilitary goods and services, and state and local expenditures all declined sharply in absolute dollar amounts despite an inflation of nearly 8 percent a year.

Some observers argue that high levels of military spending are introduced to take up the slack and maintain demand in an otherwise depression-prone economy. If this were the case, opportunity costs would be minimal. But there is little evidence for that proposition in the American experience of recent decades. Certainly the Vietnam experience does not support it. I assume, *pace* "Iron Mountain," that with the demonstrable public and private needs of this society, and with modern tools of economic analysis and manipulation, full or near-full employment of resources would be maintained even in the face of major cuts in military spending. Because of the skill with which economic systems are now managed in modern economies, defense expenditures are much more likely to force trade-offs than they were some 30 years ago. Hence the point of my original question, "Who pays for defense?"

I do not argue that defense expenditures are necessarily without broader social utility. Spending for military research and development produces important (if sometimes overrated) technological spill-overs into the civilian sector. The education, skills and physical conditioning that young men obtain during service in the armed forces are likely to benefit them and their society when they return to civilian life. Nevertheless the achievement of such benefits through spill-overs is rarely the most efficient way to obtain them. While scientific research may be serendipitous, the odds are far better that a new treatment for cancer will come from medical research than from work on missile systems. Therefore we must still consider as real costs the trade-offs that appear when defense cuts deep into the GNP, though they are not quite so heavy as a literal interpretation of the dollar amounts would imply.

One must also recognize that some civilian expenditures —for health, for education and for research—have been stimulated by Cold War and ultimately military requirements. Such were various programs of the 1950s, when a greater need was felt for a long-run girding of the loins than for more immediate military capabilities. Still, to concede this is far from undercutting the relevance of the kind of question we shall be asking. If civilian and military expenditures consistently compete for scarce resources, then the one will have a negative effect on the other; if both are driven by the same demands, they will be positively correlated. If they generally compete but are sometimes viewed as complementary, the negative correlation will be fairly low.

An evaluation of the relationship of defense and alternative kinds of spending in this country requires some explicit criteria. There is room for serious argument about what those criteria should be, but I will suggest the following:

1. It is bad to sacrifice future productivity and resources for current preparation for war or war itself; insofar as possible such activities should be financed out of current consumption. Such an assumption might be easily challenged if it were offered as a universal, but for the developed countries of North America and Western Europe in recent years it seems defensible. All of them are now, relative to their own past and to other nations' present, extremely affluent, with a high proportion of their resources flowing into consumption in the private sector. Furthermore, for most of the years 1938-1968, the demands of defense have not been terribly great. Since the end of

World War II, none of these countries has had to devote more than about 10 percent of its GNP to military needs, save for the United States during the Korean War when the figure rose to just over 13 percent. It is surely arguable that such needs rarely require substantial mortgaging of a nation's future.

a. By this criterion one would hope to see periodic up-swings in defense requirements financed largely out of personal consumption, with capital formation and such social investment in the public sector as health and education being insensitive to military demands.

b. Another aspect of this criterion, however, is that one would also anticipate that in periods of declining military needs the released resources would largely be kept for investment and education rather than returned to private consumption. In a strong form the criterion calls for a long-term increase in the proportion of GNP devoted to various forms of investment, an increase that would show up on a graph as a fluctuating line made up of a series of upward slopes followed by plateaus, insensitive to rising defense needs but responsive to the opportunities provided by relaxations in the armament pace.

2. Another point of view, partially in conflict with the last comment, would stress the need for a high degree of insulation from political shocks. A constant and enlarging commitment to the system's social resources is necessary for the most orderly and efficient growth of the system, avoiding the digestive problems produced by alternate feast and famine. Some spending, on capital expenditures for buildings for instance, may be only temporarily postponed in periods of fiscal stringency, and may bounce back to a higher level when the pressure of defense needs is eased. To that degree the damage would be reduced, but not eliminated. In the first place, school construction that

is "merely" postponed four years will come in time to help some students, but for four years a great many students simply lose out. Secondly, boom and bust fluctuations, even if they do average out to the socially desired dollar level, are likely to be inefficient and produce less real output than would a steadier effort.

Guns, Butter and Structures

Calculation of a nation's GNP is an exercise in accounting; economists define the GNP as the sum of expenditures for personal consumption, investment or capital formation, government purchases of goods and services and net foreign trade (exports minus imports). Each of these categories can be broken down. Private consumption is the sum of expenditures on durable goods (e.g., automobiles, furniture, appliances), nondurables (e.g., food, clothing, fuel) and services (airline tickets, haircuts, entertainment); investment includes fixed investment in nonresidential structures, producers' durable equipment (e.g., machinery), residential structures and the accumulation or drawing down of stocks (inventories); government purchases include both civil and military expenditures of the federal government and spending by state and local units of government. Except for inventories (which fluctuate widely in response to current conditions and are of little interest for this study) we shall look at all these, and later at a further breakdown of public expenditures by level and function.

In the table, the first column of figures—the percentage of variance explained—tells how closely defense spending and the alternate spending category vary together—how much of the changes in the latter can be "accounted for" by defense changes. The regression coefficient tells the

TABLE I: THE EFFECT OF DEFENSE SPENDING ON
CIVILIAN ACTIVITIES IN THE UNITED STATES, 1939-1968

	% of Variation	Regression Coefficient	Index of Proportionate Reduction
Personal Consumption			
Total	84	—.420	—.041
Durable Goods	78	—.163	—.123
Nondurable Goods	04	—.071	—.014
Services	54	—.187	—.050
Fixed Investment Total	72	—.292	—.144
Nonresidential Structures	62	—.068	—.140
Producers' Durable			
Equipment	71	—.110	—.123
Residential Structures	60	—.114	—.176
Exports	67	—.097	—.115
Imports	19	—.025	—.037
Federal Civil Purchases	38	—.048	—.159
State and Local Gov't			
Consumption	38	—.128	—.105

amount in dollars by which the alternate spending category changes in response to a one dollar increase in defense. The proportionate reduction index shows the damage suffered by each category relative to its "normal" base. It assumes for illustration a total GNP of $400 billion, an increase of $25 billion in defense-spending from the previous period, and that the alternative expenditure category had previously been at that level represented by its mean percentage of GNP over the 1946-1967 period. This last measure is important for policy purposes, since the impact of the same dollar reduction will be far greater to a $100 billion investment program than to a $500 billion total for consumer-spending.

Looking at the table, one can see that, in general, the American experience has been that the consumer pays most. Guns do come at the expense of butter. Changes in defense expenditure account for 84 percent of the ups and downs in total personal consumption, and the regression coefficient is a relatively high –.420. That is, a one dollar rise in defense expenditures will, all else being equal, result in a decline of $.42 in private consumption.

Of the subcategories, sales of consumer durables are most vulnerable, with 78 percent of their variations accounted for by defense. Spending on services is also fairly vulnerable to defense expenditures, with the latter accounting for 54 percent of the variance. But the negative effect of defense spending on nondurables is not nearly so high, with only 4 percent of the variance accounted for. This is not surprising, however, as needs for nondurables are almost by definition the least easily postponed. Moreover, during the World War II years new consumer durables such as automobiles and appliances were virtually unavailable, since the factories that normally produced them were then turning out war material. Similarly, due to manpower shortages almost all services were expensive and in short supply, and long-distance travel was particularly discouraged ("Is this trip necessary?"). Hence, to the degree that the consumers' spending power was not mopped up by taxes or saved, an unusually high proportion was likely to go into nondurables.

Investment (fixed capital formation) also is typically hard-hit by American war efforts and, because it means a smaller productive capacity in later years, diminished investment is a particularly costly loss. Defense accounted for 72 percent of the variations in investment, which is only a little less than that for defense on consumption, and the reduction of $.292 in investment for every $1.00 rise in defense is substantial. The coefficient is of course much lower than that for defense and consumption (with a coefficient of –.420) but that is very deceptive considering the "normal" base from which each starts. Over the 30 years for which we have the figures, consumption took a mean percentage of GNP that was typically about five times as great as investment. Thus in our hypothetical illustration a $25 billion increase in defense costs in a GNP of $400 billion would, *ceteris paribus,* result in a drop in consumption from approximately $256 billion to roughly $245 billion or only a little over 4 percent of total consumption. Investment, on the other hand, would typically fall from $51 billion to about $44 billion, or more than 14 percent. Proportionately, therefore, investment is much harder hit by an expansion of the armed services than is consumption. Since future production is dependent upon current investment, the economy's future resources and power base are thus much more severely damaged by the decision to build or employ current military power than is current indulgence. According to some rough estimates, the marginal productivity of capital in the United States is between 20 and 25 percent; that is, an additional dollar of investment in any single year will produce 20-25 cents of annual additional production in perpetuity. Hence if an extra billion dollars of defense in one year reduced investment by $292 million, thenceforth the level of output in the economy would be permanently diminished by a figure on the order of $65 million per year.

This position is modified slightly by the detailed breakdown of investment categories. Residential structures (housing) vary less closely with defense spending than do nonhousing structures or durable goods for producers, but its regression coefficient is the strongest and shows that it takes the greatest proportionate damage. Within the general category of investment, therefore, nonresidential structures and equipment usually hold up somewhat better proportionately than does housing. Doubtless this is the result of deliberate public policy, which raises home interest rates and limits the availability of mortgages while trying at the same time to maintain an adequate flow of capital to those firms needing to convert or expand into military production.

The nation's international balance of payments is often a major casualty of sharp increases in military expenditures; the present situation is not unusual. Some potential exports are diverted to satisfy internal demand, others are lost because domestic inflation raises costs to a point where the goods are priced out of the world market. Imports may rise directly to meet the armed forces' procurement needs—goods purchased abroad to fill local American military requirements show up as imports to the national economy—and other imports rise indirectly because of domestic demand. Some goods normally purchased from domestic suppliers are not available in sufficient quantities; others, because of inflation, become priced above imported goods. If the present situation is "typical," the Vietnam war's cost to the civilian economy would be responsible for a loss of more than $1.5 billion dollars in exports.

The import picture is more complicated. According to the sketch above, imports should *rise* with defense spending, but in the table the percentage of variance explained is very low and the regression coefficient is actually negative. This, however, is deceptive. The four years of World War II show unusually low importation due to a combination of enemy occupation of normal sources of goods for the United States, surface and submarine combat in the sea lanes and the diversion of our allies' normal export industries to serve their war needs. To assess the impact of defense expenditures on imports in a less than global war one must omit the World War II data from the analysis. Doing so produces the expected rise in imports with higher defense spending, on the order of $+.060$. This suggests that the current effect of Vietnam may be to add, directly and indirectly, over $1 billion to the nation's annual import bill. Coupled with the loss of exports, the total damage to the balance of payments on current account (excluding capital transfers) is in the range $2.5–$3.0 billion. That still does not account for the entire balance of payments deficit that the United States is experiencing (recently as high as $3.4 billion annually) but it goes a long way toward explaining it.

The Public Sector

In the aggregate there is no very strong impact of defense on civil public expenditures. The amount of variation accounted for by defense is a comparatively low 38 percent; the regression coefficients are only $-.048$ for federal civil purchases and $-.013$ for state and local governments. During the four peak years of World War II changes in federal civil expenditures were essentially unrelated to changes in defense spending. Samuel P. Huntington, however, notes, "Many programs in agriculture, natural resources, labor and welfare dated back to the 1930's or middle 1940's. By the mid-1950's they had become accepted responsibilities of the government," and hence politically resistant to the arms squeeze. If so, the overall inverse relationship we do find may be masking sharper changes in some of the less well-entrenched subcategories of central government budgeting. Further masking of the impact on actual programs may stem from the inability of government agencies to reduce costs for building-maintenance and tenured employees, thus forcing them in dry times to cut other expenses disproportionately.

When relating state and local government expenditures to defense some restraint is required. There really is no relationship except between the points above and below the 15 percent mark for defense. During World War II state and local government units did have their spending activities curtailed, but overall they have not been noticeably affected by defense purchases. Quite to the contrary, spending by state and local political units has risen steadily, in an almost unbroken line, since 1944. The rise, from 3.6 percent of the GNP to 11.2 percent in 1968, has continued essentially heedless of increases or diminution in the military's demands on the economy.

When we look at the breakdowns by function, however, it becomes clear that the effect of defense fluctuations is more serious, if less distinct, than for GNP categories. I have chosen three major items—education, health and welfare—for further analysis, on the grounds that one might reasonably hypothesize for each that expenditure levels would be sensitive to military needs, and, for the first two, that a neglect of them would do serious long-term damage to the economy and social system of the nation.

All three are sensitive to defense spending, with welfare somewhat more so than the others, which is not surprising. In most of this analysis reductions in expenditure levels that are forced by expanded defense activities represent a cost to the economic and social system, but welfare is different. Insofar as the needs for welfare, rather than simply the resources allocated to it, are reduced, one cannot properly speak of a cost to the economy. Rather, if one's social preferences are for work rather than welfare, the shift represents a gain to the system. Heavy increases in military pay and procurement do mean a reduction in unemployment, and military cutbacks are often associated with at least temporary or local unemployment. The effect seems strongest on state and local governments' welfare spending. In fact, the inverse relationship between defense and welfare at most spending levels is understated at 54 percent on the chart. At all but the highest levels of defense spending achieved in World War II, the inverse relationship is very steep, with small increases in military needs having a very marked dampening effect on welfare costs. But manpower was quite fully employed during all the years of major effort in World War II, so ups and downs in defense needs during 1942-1945 had little effect.

Both for education and for health and hospitals, the relationship to the immediate requirements of national defense is less powerful (less variance is explained), but nonetheless important. Furthermore, the regression coefficient is quite high for education, and since the mean share of GNP going to education is only 3.5 percent for the period under consideration, the proportionate impact of reductions is severe.

A widespread assumption holds that public expenditures on education have experienced a long-term secular growth in the United States. That assumption is correct only with modifications. The proportion of GNP devoted to public education has increased by three quarters over the period, from 3.0 percent in 1938 to 5.3 percent in 1967. But it has by no means been a smooth and steady upward climb. World War II cut deeply into educational resources, dropping the educational percentage of GNP to 1.4 in 1944; only in 1950 did it recover to a level (3.6 percent) notably above that of the 1930s. Just at that point the Korean War intervened, and education once more suffered, not again surpassing the 3.6 percent level before 1959. Since

TABLE II: THE EFFECT OF DEFENSE SPENDING ON PUBLIC CIVIL ACTIVITIES IN THE U.S., FISCAL YEARS 1939-67

	% of Variation	Regression Coefficient	Index of Proportionate Reduction
Education—Total	35	—.077	—.139
Institutions of Higher Ed.	12	—.013	—.146
Local Schools	34	—.053	—.125
Other Ed.	19	—.014	—.265
Federal Direct to Ed.	16	—.013	—.309
Federal Aid to State & Local Gov'ts for Ed.	08	—.004	—.140
State & Local Gov't for Ed.	24	—.060	—.124
Health & Hospitals—Total	32	—.017	—.113
Total Hospitals	30	—.014	—.123
Fed. for Hospitals	25	—.004	—.130
State & Local for Hospitals	29	—.011	—.120
Other Health—Total	22	—.003	—.087
Fed. for Health	06	—.001	—.101
State & Local for Health	45	—.002	—.078
Welfare—Total	54	.019	—.128
Fed. Direct for Welfare	13	.003	—.493
Fed. Aid to State & Local Gov'ts for Welfare	17	—.005	—.087
State & Local for Welfare	30	—.011	—.134

then, however, it has grown fairly steadily without being adversely affected by the relatively modest rises in defense spending. Actually, educational needs may have benefitted somewhat from the overall decline in the military proportion of the economy that took place between the late 1950s and mid-1960s. The sensitivity of educational expenditures to military needs is nevertheless much more marked on the latter's upswings than on its declines. Education usually suffers very immediately when the military needs to expand sharply; it recovers its share only slowly after defense spending has peaked. Surprisingly, federal educational expenditures are less related (less variance explained) than is spending by state and local units of government; also, local schools at the primary and secondary levels are more sensitive than are public institutions of higher education, whose share has grown in every year since 1953.

Public expenditures for health and hospitals are only a little less sensitive to the pressures of defense than are dollars for education. Here again the image of a long-term growth deceptively hides an equally significant pattern of swings. Health and hospitals accounted for a total of .77 percent of GNP in 1938; as with education this was sharply cut by World War II and was not substantially surpassed (at 1 percent) until 1950. Once more they lost out to the exigencies of defense in the early 1950s, and bounced back slowly, at the same rate as did education, to recover the 1950 level in 1958. Since then they have continued growing slowly, with a peak of 1.23 in 1967. Thus, the pattern of health and hospitals is almost identical to that for education—some long-term growth, but great cutbacks in periods of heavy military need and only slow recovery thereafter. In detail by political unit the picture is also much the same—despite reasonable a priori expectation, federal spending for this item is less closely tied to the defense budget than is that by state and local governments. It should also be noted that the impact of defense on health and hospitals is slightly less severe than on education.

It seems fair to conclude from these data that America's most expensive wars have severely hampered the nation in its attempt to build a healthier and better-educated citizenry. (One analyst estimates that what was done to strengthen education accounted for nearly half of the United States per capita income growth between 1929 and 1957.) A long-term effort has been made, and with notable results, but typically it has been badly cut back whenever military needs pressed unusually hard.

It is too soon to know how damaging the Vietnam war will be, but in view of past patterns one would anticipate significant costs. The inability to make "investments" would leave Americans poorer, more ignorant and less healthy than would otherwise be the case. We have already seen the effect of the war on fixed capital formation. Consumption absorbed a larger absolute decline in its share of GNP between 1965 and 1968 than did fiscal investment—from 63.3 to 62.1 percent in the first instance, from 14.3 to 13.8 percent in the second; but given the much smaller base of investment, the proportionate damage is about twice as great to investment as to consumption. In most of the major categories of public social "investment," nevertheless, the record is creditable. Despite a rise from 7.6 to 9.1 percent in the defense share between 1965 and 1967, the total public education and health and hospitals expenditure shares went up 4.5 to 5.3 percent and from 1.17 to 1.23 percent respectively. And even federal spending for education and health, though not hospitals, rose. There are of course other costs involved in the inability to initiate needed programs—massive aid to the cities is the obvious example. But on maintaining or expanding established patterns of expenditure the score is not bad at all.

The pattern of federal expenditures for research and development indicates some recent but partially hidden costs to education and medicine. From 1955 to 1966 R & D expenditures rose spectacularly and steadily from $3.3

billion to $14.9 billion. Obviously such a skyrocketing growth could not continue indefinitely; not even most of the beneficiary scientists expected it to do so, and in fact the rate of increase of expenditures fell sharply as early as 1966—the first year since 1961 when the defense share of GNP showed any notable increase.

Finally, we must note a very important sense in which many of these cost estimates are substantially underestimated. My entire analysis has necessarily been done with expenditure data in current prices; that is, not adjusted for inflation. Since we have been dividing each expenditure category by GNP in current dollars that would not matter providing that price increases were uniform throughout the economy. But if prices increased faster in, say, education or health, than did prices across the board, the real level of expenditure would be exaggerated. And as anyone who has recently paid a hospital bill or college tuition bill knows, some prices have increased faster than others. From 1950 through 1967 the cost of medical care, as registered in the consumer price index, rose by 86.2 percent. Thus even though the health and hospital share of public expenditure rose in current prices, the real share of national production bought by that spending fell slightly, from one percent to about .99 percent. Presumably the difference has been made up in the private sector, and benefits have been heavily dependent upon ability to pay. Comparable data on educational expenses are less easy to obtain, but we do know that the average tuition in private colleges and universities rose 39 percent, and in public institutions 32 percent, over the years 1957-1967. This too is faster than the cost of living increase over those years (not more than 20 percent), but not enough to wipe out a gain for government education expenditures in their share of real GNP.

In evaluating the desirability of an expanded defense effort, policy-makers must bear in mind the opportunity costs of defense, the kinds and amounts of expenditures that will be foregone. The relationships we have discovered in past American experience suggest what the costs of future military efforts may be, although these relationships are not of course immutable. Should it be concluded that certain new defense needs must be met, it is possible by careful choice and control to distribute the burdens somewhat differently. If costs cannot be avoided, perhaps they can be borne in such a way as to better protect the nation's future.

October 1969

FURTHER READING SUGGESTED BY THE AUTHOR:

Public Expenditures in Communist and Capitalistic Nations by Frederic L. Pryor (Homewood, Ill.: Irwin, 1969) is an important work by an economist and contains a major chapter on military expenditures in many countries.

The Common Defense by Samuel P. Huntington (New York: Columbia, 1961) needs updating but is still a valuable examination of the degree and kind of political supervision of military spending in the United States.

"Who Pays for Defense?" by Bruce M. Russett (*American Political Science Review,* 63, June 1969) contains material from this essay but also a comparison of the American experience with that in Britain, Canada and France.

The Pentagon Papers
and Social Science

IRVING LOUIS HOROWITZ

Today, no major political event, particularly one so directly linked to the forging of American foreign policy as the publication of the Pentagon Papers by the *New York Times* and the *Washington Post* can be fully described without accounting for the role of the social scientist. In this case, the economists clearly performed a major role. From the straightforward hawkish prescriptions offered in 1961 by Walt W. Rostow to the dovishly motivated release of secret documents on the conduct of the war in 1971 by Daniel Ellsberg, the contributions of social scientists were central. As a consequence, it is fitting, nay imperative, that the import of these monumental events be made plain for those of us involved in the production and dissemination of social science information and insight.

The publication of the Pentagon Papers is of central importance to the social science community in at least two respects: social scientists participated in the development of a posture and position toward the Vietnam involvement; and at a more abstract level, the publication of these papers provides lessons about political participation and policy-making for the social sciences.

We live in an age in which the social sciences perform a special and unique role in the lives of men and in the fates of government, whatever be the status of social science theory. And because the questions of laymen are no longer, Is social science scientific? but, What kinds of recommendations are offered in the name of social science? it is important that social scientists inquire as to any special meaning of the Pentagon Papers and documents, over and above the general and broad-ranging discussions that take place in the mass media. Thus, my effort here is not to be construed as a general discussion of issues, but rather a specific discussion of results.

I. Findings

The Pentagon's project director for a *History of United States Decision-Making Process on Vietnam Policy* (more simply known as *The Pentagon Papers*), economist Leslie H. Gelb now of Brookings, remarked: "Writing history, especially where it blends into current events, especially where the current event is Vietnam, is a treacherous exercise." Former Secretary of Defense Robert S. McNamara authorized this treacherous exercise of a treacherous conflict in 1967. In initiation and execution this was to be "encyclopedic and objective." The actual compilation runs to 2.5 million words and 47 volumes of narrative and documents. And from what has thus far been made public, it is evident that this project was prepared with the same bloodless, bureaucratic approach that characterizes so much federally inspired social science and history. The Pentagon

Papers attempt no original hypothesis, provide no insights into the behavior of the "other side," make scant effort to select important from trivial factors in the escalation process; they present no real continuity with past American foreign policy and in general eschew any sort of systematic survey research or interviewing of the participants and proponents. Yet, with all these shortcomings, these materials offer a fascinating and unique account of how peace-keeping agencies became transformed into policy-making agencies. That this record was prepared by 36 political scientists, economists, systems analysts, inside dopesters and outside social science research agencies provides an additional fascination: how the government has learned to entrust its official records to mandarin types, who in exchange for the cloak of anonymity are willing to prepare an official record of events. An alarming oddity is that, in part at least, the chronicle was prepared by analysts who were formerly participants.

For those who have neither the time nor the patience to examine every document thus far released, it might be worthwhile to simply summarize what they contain. In so doing, it becomes clear that the Vietnam War was neither a Democratic nor a Republican war, but a war conducted by the political elite, often without regard to basic technical advice and considerations, and for reasons that had far less to do with curbing communism than with the failure of the other arms of government in their responsibility to curb executive egotism. The publication of these papers has chronicled this country's overseas involvement with a precision never before available to the American public. Indeed, we now know more about decision-making in Vietnam than about the processes by which we became involved in the Korean War. For instance, we have learned that:

1. The United States ignored eight direct appeals for aid from Ho Chi Minh in the first half-year following World War II. Underlying the American refusal to deal with the Vietnamese leader was the growth of the Cold War and the opposition to assisting a communist leadership.

2. The Truman administration, by 1949 had already accepted the "domino principle," after the National Security Council was told early in 1950 that the neighboring countries of Thailand and Burma could be expected to fall under communist control if Vietnam were controlled by a communist-dominated regime.

3. The Eisenhower administration, particularly under the leadership of Secretary of State John Foster Dulles, refused to accept the Geneva accords ending the French-Indochina war on the grounds that it permitted this country "only a limited influence" in the affairs of the fledgling South Vietnam. Indeed, the Joint Chiefs of Staff opted in favor of displacing France as the key influence rather than assisting the termination of hostilities.

4. The final years of the Eisenhower administration were characterized by a decision to commit a relatively small number of United States military personnel to maintain the Diem regime in Saigon and to prevent a détente between Hanoi and Saigon.

5. The Kennedy administration transformed the limited-risk gamble into an unlimited commitment. Although the troop levels were indeed still quite limited, the Kennedy administration moved special forces units into Vietnam, Laos and Cambodia—thus broadening the conflict to the area as a whole.

6. The Kennedy administration knew about and ap-

proved of plans for the military coup d'état that overthrew President Diem. The United States gave its support to an army group committed to military dictatorship and no compromise with the Hanoi regime.

7. The Johnson administration extended the unlimited commitment to the military regime of Saigon. Under this administration between 1965 and 1968, troop levels surpassed 500,000 and United States participation was to include the management of the conflict and the training of the ARVN.

8. After the Tet offensive began in January 1968, Johnson, under strong prodding from the military Chiefs of Staff, and from his field commanders, moved toward full-scale mobilization, including the call-up of reserves. By the termination of the Johnson administration, the United States had been placed on a full-scale war footing.

Among the most important facts revealed by the Papers is that the United States first opposed a settlement based on the Geneva accords, signed by all belligerents; that the United States had escalated the conflict far in advance of the Gulf of Tonkin incident and had used congressional approval for legitimating commitments already undertaken rather than as a response to new communist provocations; and finally that in the face of internal opposition from the same Department of Defense that at first had sanctioned the war, the executive decided to disregard its own policy advisers and plunge ahead in a war already lost.

II. Decisions

Impressive in this enumeration of policy decisions is the clinical way decisions were made. The substitution of war game thinking for any real political thinking, the total submission of the Department of State to the Department of Defense in the making of foreign policy, and the utter collapse of any faith in compromise, consensus or coopera- tion between nations, and the ludicrous pursuit of victory (or at least non-defeat) in Vietnam, all are so forcefully illustrated in these Pentagon Papers, that the vigor with which their release was opposed by the Attorney General's office and the executive branch of government generally, can well be appreciated.

Ten years ago in writing *The War Game* I had occa- sion to say in a chapter concerning "American Politics and Military Risks" that "a major difficulty with the thinking of the new civilian militarists is that they study war while ignoring politics." The recent disclosure of the Pentagon Papers bears out that contention with a vengeance; a kind of hot-house scientology emerges, in which the ends of foreign policy are neatly separated from the instruments of immediate destruction. That a certain shock and cynicism have emerged as a result of the revelations in these papers is more attributable to the loss of a war than to the novelty of the revelations. The cast of characters that have dragged us through the mire of a bloody conflict in Southeast Asia, from Walt W. Rostow to Henry A. Kissinger, remain to haunt us and taunt us. They move in and out of admin- istrations with an ease that belies political party differences and underscores the existence of not merely a set of "experts," but rather a well-defined ruling class dedicated to manufacturing and manipulating political formulas.

The great volume of materials thus far revealed is characterized by few obvious themes: but one of the more evident is the utter separation of the purposes of devasta- tion from comprehension of the effects of such devastation. A kind of Howard Johnson sanitized vision of conflict emerges that reveals a gulf between the policy-makers and battlefield soldiers that is even wider and longer than the distance between Saigon and Washington. If the concept of war gaming is shocking in retrospect, this is probably due more to its utter and contemptible failure to provide battlefield victories than to any real development in social and behavioral science beyond the shibboleths of decision theory and game theory.

III. "Scientists"

A number of researchers as well as analysts of the Pentagon Papers were themselves social scientists. There were political scientists of considerable distinction, such as Morton Halperin and Melvin Gurtov; economists of great renown, such as Walt W. Rostow and Daniel Ellsberg; and systems analysts, such as Alain Enthoven. And then there was an assorted group of people, often trained in law, such as Roger Fisher and Carl Kaysen, weaving in and out of the Papers, providing both point and counterpoint. There are the thoroughly hawkish views of Walt Rostow; and the cautionary perspective of Alain Enthoven; and the more liberal recommendations of people like Roger Fisher. But it is clear that social scientists descend in importance as they move from hawk to dove. Walt Rostow is a central figure, and people like Carl Kaysen and Roger Fisher are at most peripheral consultants—who in fact, seem to have been more often conservatized and impressed by the pressurized Washington atmosphere than to have had an impact on the liberalization or softening of the Vietnam posture.

The social scientific contingency in the Pentagon, whom I christened the "new civilian militarists" a decade ago, were by no means uniform in their reactions to the quagmire in Vietnam. Political scientists like Morton H. Halperin and economists like Alain Enthoven did provide cautionary responses, if not outright criticisms of the repeated and incessant requests for troop build-ups. The Tet offensive, which made incontrovertible the vulnerability of the American posture, called forth demands for higher troop levels on the part of Generals William C. Westmoreland and Maxwell Taylor. Enthoven, in particular, opposed this emphatically and courageously:

> Our strategy of attrition has not worked. Adding 206,000 more U.S. men to a force of 525,000, gaining only 27 additional maneuver battalions and 270 tactical fighters at an added cost to the U.S. of $10 billion per year raises the question of who is making it costly for whom. . . . We know that despite a massive influx of 500,000 U.S. troops, 1.2 million tons of bombs a year, 200,000 enemy killed in action in three years, 20,000 U.S. killed in action in three years, 200,000 U.S. wounded in action, etc., our control of the countryside and the defense of the urban areas is now essentially at pre-August 1965 levels. We have achieved stalemate at a high commitment. A new strategy must be sought.

Interestingly, in the same month, March 1968, when Enthoven prepared this critical and obviously sane report, he wrote a curious paper on "Thomism and the Concept of Just and Unjust Warfare," which, in retrospect, seemed to be Enthoven's way of letting people like myself know that he was a dissenting voice despite his earlier commitment to war game ideology and whiz-kid strategy.

As a result of these memoranda, Assistant Defense Secretary Paul Warnke argued against increased bombing and for a bombing pause. He and Assistant Secretary of Defense for Public Affairs, Phil G. Goulding, were then simply directed to write a draft that "would deal only with the troop issue"; hence forcing them to abandon the internal fight against an "expansion of the air war." And as it finally went to the White House, the report was bleached of any criticism. The mandarin role of the social scientists was reaffirmed: President Johnson's commitments went unchallenged. The final memo advocated deployment of 22,000 more troops, reserved judgment on the deployments of the remaining 185,000 troops and approved a 262,000 troop reserve build-up; it urged no new peace initiatives and simply declared that a division of opinion existed on the bombing policy, making it appear that the division in opinion was only tactical in nature. As the Pentagon Papers declared:

> Faced with a fork in the road of our Vietnam policy, the working group failed to seize the opportunity to change directions. Indeed, they seemed to recommend that we continue rather haltingly down the same road, meanwhile, consulting the map more frequently and in greater detail to insure that we were still on the right road.

One strange aspect of this war game strategy is how little the moves and motives of the so-called "other side" were ever taken into account. There is no real appreciation of the distinction between North Vietnam and the National Liberation Front of South Vietnam. There is not the slightest account taken of the actual decisions made by General Giap or Chairman Ho. The Tet offensive seems to have taken our grand strategists by as much surprise as the political elites whom they were planning for. While they were beginning to recognize the actual balance of military forces, Wilfred Burchett had already declared, in 1967 to be exact, that the consequences of the war were no longer in doubt—United States involvement could not forestall a victory of the communist factions North and South. Thus, not only do the Pentagon Papers reveal the usual ignorance of the customs, languages and habits of the people being so brutally treated, but also the unanticipated arrogance of assuming throughout that logistics would conquer all. Even the doves like George W. Ball never doubted for a moment that an influx of a certain number of United States troops would in fact swing the tide of battle the way that General Westmoreland said it would. The argument was rather over tactics: Is such a heavy investment worth the end results? In fact, not one inner circle "wise man" raised the issue that the size of the troop commitment might be basically irrelevant to the negative (from an American viewpoint) outcome of the Southeast Asian operations. One no longer expects good history or decent ethnography from those who advise the rulers, but when this is compounded with a heavy dose of impoverished war gaming and strategic thinking in the void, then the question of "science for whom" might well be converted into the question of "what science and by whom."

All of this points up a tragic flaw in policy-making by social science experts. Their failure to generate or to reflect a larger constituency outside of themselves made them continually vulnerable to assaults from the military and from the more conservative sectors of the Pentagon. This vulnerability was so great that throughout the Pentagon Papers, one senses that the hawk position is always and uniformly outspoken and direct, while the dove position is always and uniformly ubiquitous and indirect. The basis of democratic politics has always been the mass participation of an informed electorate. Yet it was precisely this informed public, where a consensus against the war had been building, that was cut off from the policy-planners and recommenders. Consequently they were left in pristine isolation to pit their logic against the crackpot realism of their military adversaries within the bowels of government.

IV. Disclosures

Certain serious problems arose precisely because of the secrecy tag: for example, former Vice President Hubert Humphrey and Secretary of State Dean Rusk have both denied having any knowledge whatsoever of these papers. Dean Rusk went so far as to say that the research methodology was handled poorly: "I'm rather curious about why the analysts who put this study together did not interview us, particularly when they were attributing attitudes and motives to us." (*New York Times,* Saturday, July 3, 1971.) Perhaps more telling is Dean Rusk's suggestion that the Pentagon Papers have the characteristics of an anonymous letter. Along with Dean Rusk, I too believe that the names of the roughly 40 scholars connected with the production of these papers should be published. To do otherwise would not only prevent the people involved from checking the veracity of the stories attributed to them, but more important, would keep the social science community from gaining a clearer insight into the multiple roles of scholars, researchers, professors and government analysts and policy-makers. The nature of science requires that the human authorities behind these multi-volumes be identified, as in the precedent established by the identification of the authors of the various bombing surveys done after World War II and the Korean War.

One serendipitous consequence of the Pentagon Papers has been to provide a more meaningful perspective toward the proposed "Code of Ethics" being advanced by so many social science professional associations. They all deal with the sanctity of the "subject's rights." All sorts of words guarding privacy are used: "rights of privacy and dignity," "protection of subjects from personal harm," "preservation

of confidentiality of research data." The American Sociological Association proposals for example are typical:

Confidential information provided by a research subject
must be treated as such by the sociologist. Even though
research information is not a privileged communication
under the law, the sociologist must, as far as possible,
protect subjects and informants. Any promises made to
such persons must be honored. . . . If an informant or
other subject should wish, however, he can formally
release the promise of confidentiality.

While the purpose of this code of ethics is sincerely
geared to the protection of individuals under study, if taken
literally, a man like Daniel Ellsberg would be subject to
penalty, if not outright expulsion, on the grounds that he
was never allowed by the individuals concerned to make
his information public. What so many professional societies
forget is that the right to full disclosure is also a principle,
just as significant as the right of the private subject to
confidentiality, and far more germane to the tasks of a
social scientific learned society. The truly difficult ethical
question comes not with the idea of maintaining confidentiality, but with determining what would be confidential,
and when such confidentiality should be violated in terms
of a higher principle. All social science codes of ethics
presume an ethical standpoint which limits scientific endeavor, but when it is expedient to ignore or forget this
ethical code, as in the case of the Pentagon Papers, the
profession embarrassingly chooses to exhibit such a memory lapse. The publication of the Pentagon Papers should
once again point the way to the highest obligation of social
science organizations: to the truth, plain and simple, rather
than the preservation of confidentiality, high and mighty.
And unless this lesson is fully drawn, a dichotomous arrangement will be made between making public the docu-

ments of public servants whose policies they disapprove of and keeping private the documentation on deviants whom supposedly the social scientists are concerned with protecting. This is not an ethical approach but an opportunistic approach. It rests on political and professional expediency. The need therefore is to reassert the requisites of science for full disclosure, and the ethics of full disclosure as the only possible ethics for any group of professional scientists. If the release of the Pentagon Papers had done nothing else, it has reaffirmed the highest principle of all science: full disclosure, full review of the data, full responsibility for what is done, by those who do the research.

V. Secrets

Another area that deeply concerns the social scientist and that is highlighted in the Pentagon Papers is the government's established norms of secrecy. While most officials in government have a series of work norms with which to guide their behavior, few forms of anticipatory socialization have applied to social scientists who advise government agencies. The professionalization of social scientists has normally been directed toward publicity rather than secrecy. This fosters sharp differences in opinion and attitudes between the polity and the academy, since the reward system for career advancement is so clearly polarized.

The question of secrecy is intimately connected with matters of policy, because the standing assumption of policy-makers (particularly in the field of foreign affairs) is not to reveal themselves entirely. No government in the game of international politics feels that its policies can be candidly revealed for full public review; therefore, operational research done in connection with policy considerations is customarily bound by the canons of government privacy. But while scientists have a fetish for publicizing their information as a mechanism for professional advancement no less than as a definition of their essential role in the society, the political branches of society have as their fetish the protection of private documents and privileged information. Therefore, the polity places a premium not only on acquiring vital information, but on maintaining silence about such information precisely to the degree that the data might be of high decisional value. This leads to differing premiums between analysts and policy-makers and to tensions between them.

Social scientists complain that the norm of secrecy often-times involves yielding their own essential work premises. A critical factor reinforcing an unwilling acceptance of the norm of secrecy by social scientists is the allocation of most government research funds for military or semi-military purposes. Senate testimony has shown that 70 percent of federal funds targeted for the social sciences involve such restrictions.

The real wonder turns out to be not the existence of the secrecy norm but the relative availability of large chunks of information. Indeed, the classification of materials is so inept that documents (such as the Pax America research) designated as confidential or secret by one agency may often be made available as a public service by another agency. There are also occasions when documents placed in a classified category by sponsoring government agencies can be gotten without charge from the private research institute doing the work.

But the main point is that the norm of secrecy makes it extremely difficult to separate science from patriotism and hence makes it that much more difficult to question the research design itself. Social scientists often express the nagging doubt that accepting the first stage—the right of the government to maintain secrecy—often carries with it acquiescence in a later stage—the necessity for silence on the part of social researchers who may disagree with the political uses of their efforts.

The demand for government secrecy has a telling impact on the methodology of the social sciences. Presumably social scientists are employed because they, as a group, represent objectivity and honesty. Social scientists like to envision themselves as a wall of truth off which policy-makers may bounce their premises. They also like to think that they provide information which cannot be derived from sheer public opinion. Thus, to some degree social scientists consider that they are hired or utilized by government agencies because they will say things that may be unpopular but nonetheless significant. However, since secrecy exists, the premises upon which most social scientists seek to work are strained by the very agencies which contract out their need to know.

The terms of research and conditions of work tend to demand an initial compromise with social science methodology. The social scientist is placed in a cognitive bind. He is conditioned not to reveal maximum information lest he become victimized by the federal agencies that employ his services. Yet he is employed precisely because of his presumed thoroughness, impartiality and candor. The social scientist who survives in government service becomes circumspect or learns to play the game. His value to social science becomes seriously jeopardized. On the other hand, once he raises these considerations, his usefulness to the policy-making sector is likewise jeopardized.

Social scientists believe that openness is more than meeting formal requirements of scientific canons; it is also a matter of making information universally available. The norm of secrecy leads to selective presentation of data. The social scientist is impeded by the policy-maker because of contrasting notions about the significance of data and the general need for replication elsewhere and by others. The policy-maker who demands differential access to findings considers this a normal return for the initial expenditure of risk capital. Since this utilitarian concept of data is alien to the scientific standpoint, the schism between the social scientist and the policy-maker becomes pronounced precisely at the level of openness of information and accessibility to the work achieved. The social scientist's general attitude is that sponsorship of research does not entitle any one sector to benefit unduly from the findings—that sponsorship by federal agencies ought not place greater limitations on the use of work done than sponsorship by either private agencies or universities.

VI. Loyalties

A major area that deeply concerns social scientists is that of dual allegiance. The Pentagon Papers have such specific requirements and goal-oriented tasks that they intrude upon the autonomy of the social scientist by forcing upon him choices between dual allegiances. The researcher is compelled to choose between participating fully in the world of the federal bureaucracy or remaining in more familiar academic confines. He does not want the former to create isolation in the latter. Thus, he often criticizes the federal bureaucracy's unwillingness to recognize his basic needs: 1) the need to teach and retain full academic identity; 2) the need to publicize information; and above all 3) the need to place scientific responsibility above the call of patriotic obligation—when they may happen to clash. In short, he does not want to be plagued by dual or competing allegiances.

The norm of secrecy exacerbates this problem. Although many of the social scientists who become involved with federal research are intrigued by the opportunity to address important issues, they are confronted by some bureaucracies which oftentimes do not share their passion for resolving social problems. For example, federal obligations commit the bureaucracy to assign high priority to items having military potential and effectiveness and low priorities to many supposedly idealistic and far-fetched themes in which social scientists are interested.

Those social scientists, either as employees or as consultants connected with the government, are hamstrung by federal agencies which are in turn limited by political circumstances beyond their control. A federal bureaucracy must manage cumbersome, overgrown committees and data-gathering agencies. Federal agencies often protect a status quo merely for the sake of rational functioning. They must conceive of academicians in their midst as a standard bureaucratic type entitled to rise to certain federal ranks. Federal agencies limit innovating concepts to what is immediately useful, not out of choice and certainly not out of resentment of the social sciences but from what is deemed as impersonal necessity. This has the effect of reducing the social scientist's role in the government to that of ally or advocate rather than innovator or designer. Social scientists begin to feel that their enthusiasm for rapid change is unrealistic, considering how little can be done by the government bureaucracy. And they come to resent involvement in theoryless application to immediacy foisted on them by the "new utopians," surrendering in the process the value of confronting men with the wide range of choices of what might be done. The schism, then, between autonomy and involvement is as thorough as that between secrecy and publicity, for it cuts to the quick well-intentioned pretensions at human engineering.

The problem of competing allegiances is not made simpler by the fact that many high-ranking federal bureaucrats have strong nationalistic and conservative political ideologies. This contrasts markedly with the social scientist, who comes to Washington not only with a belief in the primacy of science over patriotism but also with a definition of patriotism that is more open-ended and consciously liberal than that of most appointed officials. Hence, he often perceives the conflict to extend beyond research design and social applicability into one of the incompatible ideologies held respectively by the social scientist and entrenched Washington bureaucrats. He comes to resent the proprietary attitude of the bureaucrat toward "his" government processes. The social scientist is likely to consider his social science bias a necessary buffer against the federal bureaucracy.

VII. Elitists

The publication of the Pentagon Papers sheds new light on political pluralist and power concentrationist hypotheses. When push finally did turn to shove, President Nixon and the government officials behaved as members of a ruling class and not as leaders of their political party. President Nixon might easily have chosen to let the Democratic party take the burn and bear the brunt of the assaults for the betrayal of a public trust. Indeed the Nixon administration might have chosen to join the chorus of those arguing that the Democratic party is indeed the war party, as revealed in these documents; whereas the Republican party emerges as the party of restraint—if not exactly principle. Here was a stunning opportunity for Mr. Nixon to make political capital at a no-risk basis: by simply drawing attention to the fact that the war was constantly escalated by President Truman, who refused to bargain in good faith with Ho Chi Minh despite repeated requests, by President Kennedy, who moved far beyond anything President Eisenhower had in mind for the area, by making the fatal commitment not just to land troops but to adopt a domino theory of winning the war, by President Johnson, whose role can well be considered as nefarious: coming before the American people as a peace candidate when he had already made the fatal series of commitments to continuing escalation and warfare. That the President chose not to do so illustrates the sense of class solidarity that the political elites in this country manifest; a sense of collective betrayal of the priesthood, rather than a sense of obligation to score political points and gain political trophies. And that too should be a lesson in terms of the actual power within the political structure of a small ruling elite. Surely this must be considered a fascinating episode in its own right: the reasons are complex, but surely among them must rank the belief that Mr. Nixon behaved as a member of the ruling elite, an elite that had transcendent obligations far beyond the call of party, and that was the call of class.

One fact made clear by the Pentagon Papers is the extent to which presidentialism has become the ideology and the style in American political life. The infrequency of any reference to the judicial situation with respect to the war in Southeast Asia and the virtual absence of any reference to congressional sentiments are startling confirmations of an utter change in the American political style. If any proof was needed of the emerging imbalance between the executive and other branches of government, these papers should put such doubt to rest. The theory of checks and balances works only when there are, in fact, groups such as senators or stubborn judges who believe in the responsibility of the judiciary and legislative branches to do just that, namely, establish check and balance. In the absence of such vigor, the war in Southeast Asia became very much a series of executive actions. And this itself should give pause to the advocates of consensus theory in political science.

The failure of the Vietnam episode has resulted in a reconsideration of presidentialism as the specific contemporary variant of power elite theory. The renewed vigor of Congress, the willingness, albeit cautionary willingness, of the Supreme Court to rule on fundamental points of constitutional law, are indicative of the resurgence of pluralism. In this sense, the darkest hour of liberalism as a political style has witnessed a liberal regrouping around the theme of mass politics. Even the domestic notions of community organization and states rights are indicative of the limits of presidentialism—so that Mr. Nixon, at one and the same time, is reluctantly presiding over the swan song of presidentialism in foreign affairs, while celebrating its demise in domestic affairs. The collapse of the Vietnam War and the trends toward neo-isolationism are in fact simply the reappearance of political pluralism in a context where to go further in the concentration of political power in the presidency would in all likelihood mean the upsurge of fascism, American style. If the concept of a power elite was reconfirmed in the Pentagon Papers, so too, strangely, was the concept of political pluralism in the public response to them. The countervailing influence of the Supreme Court was clearly manifested in the ringing affirmation of the First Amendment, in the denial of the concept of prior restraint and prior punitive actions, and in the very rapidity of the decision itself. This action by the judiciary, coupled with a show of muscle on the part of the Senate and House concerning the conduct of the war, military appropriations, boondoggles and special privileges for a select handful of aircraft industries in their own way served to underscore the continued importance of the open society and the pluralistic basis of power. Even executives, such as Hubert H. Humphrey, have declared in favor of full disclosure and reiterated the principles guiding the publication of the Pentagon Papers.

Power elites operate behind a cloak of anonymity. When that cloak is lifted, an obvious impairment in the operational efficiency of elites occurs. What has happened with the release of the Pentagon Papers is precisely this collapse of anonymity, no less than secrecy. As a result, the formal apparatus of government can assert its prerogatives. This does not mean that the executive branch of government will be unable to recover from this blow at its prestige, or that it will no longer attempt to play its trump card: decision-making by executive fiat. It does mean, however, that the optimal conditions under which power elites operate have been seriously hampered. The degree of this impairment and the length of time it will obtain depend exclusively on the politics of awareness and participation, no less than the continuing pressures for lowering the secrecy levels in high-level international decision-making.

Probably the most compelling set of reasons given for President Nixon's bitter opposition to the release of the Pentagon Papers is that provided by Melvin Gurtov, one of the authors of the secret Pentagon study and an outstanding political scientist specializing in Asian affairs. He speaks of three deceits in current American Vietnamese policy: "The first and most basic deceit is the Administration's contention that we're winding down and getting out of the war." In fact, Vietnamization is a "domestic political ploy that really involves the substitution of air power for ground power." The second deceit is that "we're truly interested in seeing the prisoners of war released." Gurtov notes that "as far as this administration is concerned the prisoners of war are a political device, a device for rationalizing escalation, by saying these are acts that are necessary to show our concern for the prisoners." The third deceit "is that under the Nixon Doctrine the United States is not interested in making new commitments in Asia." In fact, the administration used the Cambodia coup "as an opportunity for creating for itself a new commitment in Southeast Asia, namely the survival of a non-Communist regime in Pnompenh." This outspoken position indicates that the defense of the power elite of the past by President Nixon might just as well be construed as a self-defense of the power elite in the present.

VIII. Conspiracies

The Pentagon Papers provide much new light on theories of power elite and power diffusion and also provide an equal measure of information on conspiracy theory. And while it is still true that conspiracy *theory* is bad theory, it is false to assert that no conspiracies exist or are not perpetrated by the government. It might indeed be the case that all governments, insofar as they are formal organizations, have secrets; and we call these secrets, conspiracies. From this point of view, the interesting question is how so few leaks resulted from an effort of such magnitude and involving so many people as setting policy in the Vietnam War. Rather than be surprised that these papers reached the public domain four to six years after the fact, one should wonder how the government was able to maintain silence on matters of such far-ranging and far-reaching consequence.

Cyrus Eaton, American industrialist and confidant of many communist leaders, indicates that the Vietnamese almost instantaneously were made aware of United States policy decisions. But I seriously doubt that they actually had copies of these materials. Rather, like the American public itself, they were informed about the decisions but not the cogitations and agitations that went into the final decision. Perhaps this is the way all governments operate; nonetheless, it is fascinating—at least this once—to be privy to the process and not simply the outcome, and to see the foibles of powerful men and not just the fables manufactured for these men after the fact.

These papers tend to underwrite the common-sensical point of view that governments are not to be trusted, and to undermine the more sophisticated interpretation that governments are dedicated to the task of maintaining democracy at home and peace abroad. As bitter as it may seem, common sense cynicism has more to recommend it than the sophisticated, well elaborated viewpoints which take literally the formal structure of government and so readily tend to dismiss the informal response to power and pressure from men at the top. The constant wavering of Lyndon B. Johnson, his bellicose defiance of all evidence and information that the bombings were not having the intended effect, followed by shock that his lieutenants like Robert McNamara changed their position at midstream (which almost constituted a bertayal in the eyes of the president) were in turn followed by a more relaxed posture and a final decision not to seek the presidency. All of this forms a human drama that makes the political process at once fascinating and frightful; fascinating because we can see the psychology of politics in action, and frightful because the presumed rationality is by no means uniformly present.

The publication of the Pentagon Papers, while a considerable victory for the rights of a free press and of special significance to all scientists who still uphold the principle of full disclosure as the norm of all political as well as scientific endeavor, is not yet a total victory for a democratic society—that can only happen when the concept of secrecy is itself probed and penetrated, and when the concept of undeclared warfare is finally and fully repudiated by the public and its representatives. The behavior of the government in its effort to suppress publication of the Pentagon Papers cannot simply be viewed as idiosyncratic, but rather as part of the structure of the American political processes in which the expert displaces the politician, and the politicians themselves become so beholden to the class of experts for information, that they dare not turn for guidance to the people they serve. For years, critics of the Vietnam War have been silenced and intimidated by the policy-makers' insistence that when all the facts were known the hawk position would be vindicated and the dove position would be violated. Many of the facts are now revealed—and the bankruptcy of the advocates of continued escalation is plain for all to see. Hopefully, this will strengthen the prospects for peace, and firm up those who, as an automatic reflex, assume the correctness of the government's position on all things military. It is to be hoped that the principle of democracy, of every person counting as one, once more becomes the source of fundamental decision-making and political discourse.

September 1971

FURTHER READING SUGGESTED BY THE AUTHOR:

The basic text is *The Pentagon Papers: The Secret History of the Vietnam War,* as published by the *New York Times.* Based on investigative reporting by Neil Sheehan. Written by Neil Sheehan, Hedrick Smith, E. W. Kenworthy and Fox Butterfield. Articles and documents edited by Gerald Gold, Allan M. Siegal and Samuel Abt. (Toronto-New York-London: Bantam Books, Inc., 1971).

In The Hawk's Nest:
An Inside Story of the
Workings of the RAND Corporation

ROBERT WOLFSON

From early summer 1963 until late summer 1965, I was a member of the research staff of the RAND Corporation in Santa Monica, California. It was a particularly interesting time to be there because during that period the RAND staff members began to differ significantly among themselves over public policy matters that had their roots in the organization's work. Both the impending détente of the early 1960s (the nuclear test ban treaty was under discussion when I started work at RAND) and the escalation of the Vietnam War (the bombing of North Vietnam and the United States troop buildup in the South were already well established by the time I left) generated sharp divisions within the corporation, although in both cases the majority was on the side of the military. Dissatisfaction about Vietnam, however, persisted and apparently extended within the staff as it has among the general population of this country, and last year it resulted in the desperate and risky action taken by Daniel Ellsberg, formerly one of RAND's brightest staff members, in releasing the Pentagon Papers to the press.

This is an account of how RAND looked and felt to one of the relatively few doves on its professional staff in that earlier, crucial period.

It is now apparent that until the mid-sixties Ellsberg, like almost all those at RAND, was perfectly satisfied with the main thrust of United States foreign policy. He accepted the notion that the use or threat of using force throughout the world was a legitimate means to the attainment of United States ends abroad. And it is yet unclear whether he now feels differently except in specific circumstances. In 1965, when he was in Vietnam for the Department of Defense, he wrote to friends that the Vietnamese were beautiful people and that the United States must continue to help them. This was at a time when we were already using napalm freely, destroying villages and setting up free-fire zones, as Ellsberg has since told us he was then beginning to learn.

In some ways, an understanding of Ellsberg is extremely helpful in understanding the RAND Corporation itself. His attitudes and his way of approaching the problems of the United States and its relationship to the world are characteristic of the most important people at RAND. He would not otherwise have won such esteem there—and later at the Pentagon.

Ellsberg's act of releasing the Pentagon Papers to the public took immense personal courage on his part— courage of a particularly unusual sort. We are impressed from childhood onward with the importance of being courageous in both the physical and spiritual sense, but we are strongly impressed with the heinousness of acting against society. And for Ellsberg, as for many of us, society and the government of the United States have been indistinguishable. Yet even in taking this extraordinary step he still seems to have been unable to shed some of the former habits which he shared with other jingoists like himself at RAND. They appeared always to know they were right. They had no visible reservations. They believed that ends justified means. The word "zealot" has been used recently to describe Ellsberg and it seems to fit. When he emerged from the courthouse after being released in the summer of 1971, he was asked by a reporter if he wasn't concerned about having to go to prison. His response was most revealing: "Wouldn't you be glad to go to prison to end this terrible war?" His reply had all the conviction of the newly converted St. Augustine realizing the errors of his former ways and expecting everyone else to follow him.

In addition, Ellsberg's position is incomplete. What seems to be bothering him primarily is that the American people were treated contemptuously by their government. That is a profoundly serious matter; but by underemphasis he seems to be saying that if the American people had been taken into their government's confidence and had approved the policy, then the war itself would have been all right. Ellsberg's opinion has not been heard on our Dominican adventure in May 1965. There was a case in which the government was more honest, although not completely so. But the public did not object and we won —and quickly. Was it, then, an acceptable move?

By comparison with the way the American people were dealt with by the Johnson administration, it could almost be said that the German people were honestly dealt with by their leaders in the 1930s and most seemed to go along with them—but that is no basis for justification of Nazi policies. Democracy is not simply a set of procedures; it must be based on some moral foundation. It was this reading of democracy as procedures and not much more— procedures that could be suspended in times judged (by some elite) to be sufficiently serious—which was characteristic of the so-called defense intellectuals who played important roles in the White House, the Pentagon, Saigon and RAND.

What was it about RAND itself or the people at RAND that generated such attitudes? That question is my central concern here, and I will also attempt to explore the danger inherent in supposing that value-free analysis of social policy can be carried out by value-free analysts in the employ of power wielders.

The nature of the danger is that, as the relationship is prolonged, the thinking of both the analysts and their employers comes to resemble one another's. Their expectations of each other, especially the employers' expectations of the analysts, change subtly. Less and less do the employers really want cool levelheaded analysis. More and more they want support for the means and objectives to which they are already committed on other grounds— perhaps irrational, perhaps unconscious, perhaps impossible to reveal for any number of reasons.

In general, analysts long in the employ of the military establishment find themselves under irresistible pressure to weight the balance in favor of the exercise of military power. This exercise may range from showing the flag threateningly all the way to thermonuclear exchange. But the military worries that without such occasional exercises its chances of maintaining position and power inside the United States are threatened. So conclusions are reached under these pressures which might not have been reached in their absence.

This relationship and these pressures—most of them

subtle but powerful—are worth exploring. To do so we turn to RAND—its history, its people and its ways of doing business.

RAND was originally formed as a special group inside the Douglas Aircraft Corporation during World War II. It was established as an independent corporate entity in 1947. Its initial commitment was to the development of analytical techniques for the formulation of air-war tactics and strategy. As time passed, it expanded its concerns into air-weapons design and testing for the Atomic Energy Commission (AEC), the formulation of quantitative analyses of bombing plans and logistical procedures, and the quantitative and nonquantitative analysis of global strategy. At the same time it was being encouraged by the air force to do basic scientific work in a number of areas related to staff interests. However, as time went on, less and less of this was acceptable to the air force and, at an accelerating pace, more and more of the air force prime contract with RAND was devoted to air force operations analyses.

RAND's staff was usually classified into two broad categories: research or scientific personnel and the so-called support staff. The former were the professional personnel who conducted the analyses, wrote the reports, held the advanced degrees—mathematicians, physicists, economists, computer scientists, meteorologists, earth scientists, astronomers, statisticians, operations analysts, engineers, philosophers and social scientists. A few of these were retired air force colonels. In the second group were the secretaries, clerks, typists, computer operators, maintenance and repair people and the security guards. A group which fell between these two included computer programmers, technical writers and librarians, editors and research assistants (most of whom, in this typical American institution, were attractive, bright, young women). Apart from these groups were the executives and administrators, most of whom had once been members of the research staff. Significantly, neither the man who was president of the corporation for its first 20 years of operation nor its sole senior vice-president had ever been members of any research staff; they had been managers at Douglas before RAND was formed.

The research staff is of primary interest for it was this work which justified RAND's existence at the Pentagon, in the White House and in the planning rooms of air commands and the aerospace industry.

Most RAND people came from one of two places—the aerospace industry or the academic world. The former were largely engineers and the latter had either come directly from academic work or tended to think of it as their long-run alternative opportunity. Many people served as academic consultants at RAND for periods of a few weeks or months at a time, especially in the summer. A significant proportion of RAND's regular full-time staff had originally come there as summer consultants or as summer interns while they were graduate students.

Until the mid-sixties, a job or consultantship at RAND was, for an academician, financially advantageous, paying better than an equivalent academic post would pay on a full-year basis and better than an equivalent government job. By the mid-sixties both academic and government salaries had undergone significant improvement, both relative and absolute, so that people were easily able to leave RAND for academic or government jobs and do as well or better financially. For the engineers, RAND salaries have always been competitive with those in the aerospace industry. However, the work at RAND tended to be more interesting, and working conditions better. For example, with almost no exceptions, it was unheard of in the aerospace industry for nonexecutive engineers to have their own offices. They worked in large groups in so-called bullpens. At RAND, however, each research staff member had his own office.

Thus, for most members of the research staff, RAND was a place that offered solid professional advantages. There were frequent illuminating seminars. Publication in professional journals and trips to professional meetings were encouraged. University people were constantly visiting RAND, and in many academic fields it was considered a favorable professional qualification to have worked there. RAND was spoken of as a quasi-academic institution. Indeed, there was talk for years (which appears now to be coming to fruition) of RAND's offering a doctorate in the field of policy analysis.

Security at RAND

RAND has always been operated as a so-called secure facility. That is, it has had to observe rules laid down by Defense Department security personnel concerning entry and egress, eligibility of personnel and the handling of files and documents. As a condition of employment, all employees of RAND were required to apply for a top secret Department of Defense security clearance. Until they had been granted a secret clearance they could not have free access to the main RAND facility but worked in the small uncleared facility and were allowed into the rest of the building only with an escort. Some people I knew spent more than a year languishing in the uncleared facility before receiving a clearance. In one case the problem was an uncle who was believed to have been a communist 25 years earlier. If it turned out that the Defense Department security people were unwilling, even under

RAND pressure, to grant a top secret clearance, then employment was terminated. These conditions also applied to most consultants.

The granting of security clearance to an individual comes after a lengthy investigation by military security. Granting the clearance implies that the recipient is judged by military security to be personally and politically reliable, emotionally stable, patriotic and not subject to blackmail, and that he is to be trusted with classified military secrets up to and including the level of sensitivity of the clearance granted.

Access to classified information is granted only if two conditions are met. First, the person requesting access must hold a clearance of at least the level of classification of the information. Second, he must formally establish, in writing and to the satisfaction of the security personnel controlling the information, the basis for his need to know the classified information. The need to know must be established in terms of objectives or interests of the United States which would thereby be furthered, as interpreted by those same security personnel.

The need to know was presumed to exist for any person employed or consulting at RAND who had the proper clearance for any piece of information at RAND. So far as I know RAND was unique in this respect. This universal, presumptively established need to know appears to have been terminated by the Secretary of Defense on July 2, 1971, after the Pentagon Papers leak was traced to RAND—despite the fact it would seem to be the Defense Department's own secretiveness that was basically at fault. Ellsberg, on leave from RAND, was assigned by the Defense Department to the team writing the history of United States involvement in Vietnam, now known as the Pentagon Papers. His increasing criticism of the United

States role in Vietnam led the Defense Department to remove him from the project and give him other duties, but they did not inform RAND of this. Hence, after his return to RAND no question was raised about his access to RAND's copy of the papers.

The reconsideration of the need to know is probably the most serious revision of RAND security procedures that has taken place, although RAND staff members are already being subjected to frequent unannounced shakedowns and inspections, both covert and overt, and the RAND security office and its procedures are undoubtedly being turned upside down by air force security people. That these changes are quite sweeping is attested to by the unexpectedly early resignation—obviously under pressure—of RAND's second president, Henry Rowen, in November 1971, apparently for reasons related to the Ellsberg episode.

What this unusual past procedure meant was that any RAND staff member who was curious about a classified document, whether or not it had anything to do with the work he was engaged in, had a good chance of seeing it simply by requesting a copy. Of course he had to know that it existed and was inside RAND. This was easy if it was a document which had originally been produced at RAND and had been formally entered into the RAND publication process. Sometimes items in this process were actually published in the usual sense, but of course they were not classified. Other items were classified and assigned a publication number and would be mentioned on the list of RAND publications circulated to everyone two or three times a month. This list was itself frequently classified because some of the titles on it were classified (though usually at a lower level than the documents they described).

However, if the classified item had been brought into

RAND from another agency or if it was produced at RAND but kept in unpublished memo or letter form, then the uninvolved person would learn about it only unofficially and might have a bit of difficulty getting a look at it. Still, it was frequently possible to see someone else's copy, and a person could get one of his own if he persisted.

Thus it was possible, because there was a great deal of fairly free lunch-hour and coffee-break conversation among RAND staff members, for someone to find out a great deal about what sorts of things were being worked on and what sorts of documents were entering or being generated at RAND.

At RAND, as at any other secure facility, visitors had to be under escort at all times. Once an acquaintance of mine brought a girlfriend to his office for a few hours one evening while he worked. At one point he had to use the men's room but spent nearly a half-hour agonizing over how to handle the situation. The girl could not enter the men's room with him, he felt, and yet he had to see that she remained escorted. After a long painful period he remembered that he could leave her at the entrance to the building which was manned 24 hours a day, seven days a week, by members of the security guard.

The security guard, like a good, well-educated mannerly police force appeared to know everyone at RAND by name. Apparently the guards' jobs required that they immediately familiarize themselves with the faces of all new people as they arrived and with the entire staff of some 1,200 in short order after their own arrival. The head of the security guard was a top-sergeant type who, on one particularly hot day, came up with a dress code: no shorts for research staff. This generated a high-school type of dress-code revolt wherein many of us went home at lunch time and returned in shorts. He lost. The chief security officer and his chief assistant, both retired naval officers, were decent, unimaginative bureaucrats. They could not have done well at military installations for they were too intelligent, but they were ideal for dealing with RAND's collection of prima donnas.

RAND Liberals

Most RAND people, when it came to domestic political and social concerns, were liberals. Recently the term has come into some disrepute and with reason. But in those days it still connoted opposition in principle to discrimination, concern for the poor, support for some significant downward redistribution of power and wealth, and a corresponding antagonism toward the concentration of power and income by the rich and by corporations. It also carried a distrust (however vague) of Neanderthalism among the military—a concern over the amount of killing power in the hands of the major world military leaders. Most of all, to be a liberal placed one squarely in the pragmatic rationalist tradition—a liberal could rest comfortably when logic and analysis were being applied to human problems.

Many RAND people belonged to clubs of the California Democratic Council, the left wing of the Democratic Party in California. Many others were active in the regular Democratic Party. Only a very few considered themselves right of center. During the 1964 election campaign there were a few Goldwater bumper strips in the RAND parking lot, most of them on cars belonging to members of the support staff. The research staff had a small number of hardliners. They felt outnumbered and subject to silent ridicule, and they expressed themselves vociferously on occasion. One might have expected that it would be these people who would be staffing studies of first strike (pre-emptive) nuclear war strategy but this was not the case. The majority of people working on such studies called themselves liberals. This sort of discovery was particularly shocking.

In the Los Angeles metropolitan area the semi-informed general public spoke of RAND in hushed tones and tended automatically to regard its staff as geniuses. In truth, as a group RAND people were as brilliant and as dull, as responsible and as irresponsible, as honorable and as dishonest, as the faculty of an average large American university. The difference was that as a group they have always had more obvious and more efficient channels for transmission of their ideas into the real centers of American power. Occasionally we would encounter people who saw RAND as a keystone in the structure of Defense Department planning, who would speak in very hostile tones—and in retrospect who could blame them? In such circumstances my response was to try to explain that not all of us were planning wars, but that, while true, was not very persuasive.

A particular critic of the United States Cold War commitments, who was pleased at the development of the détente and disturbed about Vietnam, was the man in charge of public relations for RAND—although the way in which he handled his job and kept the organization out of the papers led me to describe him as RAND's public nonrelations chief. One of his activities was to invite people from the academic world and from the Left who were in the Santa Monica area to come and speak at RAND and then meet with small groups. The idea was to convince them that RAND people did not necessarily each have horns and a tail. Among those who got this treatment was Sidney Lens, the left-wing union leader who subsequently became a cochairman of the New Mobe which organized several of the most successful antiwar marches between 1967 and 1969. Norman Thomas also came and delivered a quiet but sharp attack on the war. After his speech there was an ovation and near demonstration for him in the lecture hall; I cannot recall any other person getting such a reception. Of course, it was not for his speech, but because he was Norman Thomas. For most of the RAND liberals and welfare statists he was a household symbol, impotent but important.

RAND people tended to work and play together. And their play reflected attitudes and skills carried over from their work. Competition between tennis players as well as skill at the game were at higher levels than I can recall at a half-dozen large university campuses. Extended relationships were conducted across chessboards and bridge and poker tables. Some RAND people made a near fetish of playing poker skillfully and for high stakes—the use of the bluff and high stakes was not just a part of the poker game but consciously reflected the use of the bluff and high stakes in the international strategy so many RAND people were analyzing and planning.

At noontime many of the staff members would eat lunch in several of the conference rooms. One was traditionally set aside for bridge players, another for players of Kriegspiel, a game based on chess, but in which neither player can see his opponent. Each has his own board, and the men and boards are separated by a barrier. A referee, whose job is no mean trick of visualization and analysis, checks each board and decides if a player's move is, by chess rules, legal or not. Small amounts of information are given: whether or not someone has been placed in check and if so, from what direction; whether a pawn or a piece (not further identified) has been lost and if so on what square; whether or not there are opportunities for capture by pawns and if so, on what squares. Aside from this each player is forced to hypothesize and run risks by testing his hypotheses. (Some skillful shoulder-readers used what body movement was visible over a shoulder-high barrier to generate hypotheses, so the barrier was raised.) The result is a much faster game than chess and one very different from it. It is particularly impressive to the novice observer. If there was a visitor in the house during the lunch hour he would be brought into the Kriegspiel room to watch us as we played and presumably would go out dazzled by the geniuses at RAND.

The RAND Corporation is almost invariably coupled in the popular mind with the theory of games. This is somewhat misleading. Game theory, strictly speaking, is a mathematical theory dealing with the behavior of competitive players under a very specific set of behavioral assumptions. It happens that there were at RAND a number of mathematicians concerned with the theory of games in this very restricted sense. However, other methods of analysis and other problems were the basis of most people's work there. RAND dealt, in a wide variety of contexts and with a range of methods, with problems of conflict. At the most abstract level game theory and extensions of it were explored to see if it might be possible, by developing a sufficiently rich range of conditions under which abstract mathematical models of conflict could lead to solutions, to deal with real problems of war and threat. In fact, after 20 years of this sort of research at RAND and elsewhere, game theory has yielded up few useful results.

War gaming, which is a variety of role playing with a skeletal script built around a real or hypothetical international conflict situation, has been used at RAND. In this procedure each of several persons is given a description of a role he is to play, a description of the relevant features of the situation at the beginning of play, and some information about those with and against whom he is playing. Each player makes decisions within the competence of his role in response to information he receives about the effects of his and his fellow players' decisions. In a particular game the characters would usually include high military and political figures of two opposing countries, and the cast occasionally included high-ranking civilians or military people from the Pentagon. The objectives of such a game can be both instructional for potential decision-makers and exploratory for researchers who are trying to gain insight into the structure of decision-making in particular circumstances.

Most significant at RAND in the study of conflict situations has been historical and literary analysis which consciously attempts to be rigorously (albeit not formally) logical in drawing implications of various stances of the United States and other world powers. The logical underpinnings of the entire strategy of nuclear deterrence, the face we have presented to other world superpowers for over 20 years, were worked out in this fashion, and to a significant degree at RAND. RAND's work in the planning and justification of counterinsurgency tactics and pacifiication programs carried out in Vietnam was also conducted with these techniques.

The remainder of RAND's military work has been concerned chiefly with economizing on air force procurement and operations, given the strategic commitments already worked out. These economizing studies have dealt with a wide range of matters from weapons design and testing through weapons procurement, maintenance, repair and supply. One of RAND's major studies in the fifties was concerned with such a question: Would it be better for the air force to continue to operate its Strategic Air Command bombers from overseas bases in Spain, Okinawa, North

Africa and Turkey or to develop airborne refueling and other techniques to allow SAC to operate from much less vulnerable North American bases? The study concluded that the latter course made more sense on the basis of detailed and abstract cost analyses. The air force significantly modified earlier plans it had made in response to the results.

A small fraction of RAND's work, some 10 to 15 percent when I was there, was for other government agencies or for other United States armed forces. Approximately 7 percent was sponsored by foundations and by RAND itself and was concerned with such matters as urban transportation and planning problems, aspects of theoretical biology, competer-language development and computer system design and application, computer simulation of human problem-solving activity, earth science and meteorology, international economic relations and mathematics.

RAND's only output was, as someone put it, paper —that is, reports. There were no laboratories there and all work done was theoretical, historical or computational.

Power Trips at RAND

Throughout my stay at RAND I was aware that for some people the real kick in being there came from the feeling of being involved in making important decisions. These were the relatively few people who made a trip or two to the Pentagon each month to brief high-ranking officials on the results of their studies. Some of these people would return and speak casually of "when I saw Curt LeMay last week" or "the last time I briefed the Secretary." Being at RAND was a real power trip for them. Most were working on studies of preemptive war, the use of nuclear threats against entire nations or the use of civilian populations as pawns in counterinsurgency situations. When asked how they could morally justify doing such work, several sorts of answers were forthcoming. One was the classic Eichmann excuse: "I was only doing my job, someone has to do it"; another was that these were simply contingency plans—although I never did receive an explanation of what the contingency was that could justify starting a thermonuclear war.

In the fall of 1963 an announcement was circulated of a classified (secret) meeting at which one of RAND's physicists who had long been a key figure in AEC's program of design and testing of nuclear warheads would discuss the Test Ban Treaty, then under discussion in the Senate. The lecture hall was crowded and on the lectern was a large sign: SECRET. We heard this man tell us that the United States should not sign the treaty since it would interfere with our testing our own missile emplacements' vulnerability to attack by thermonuclear warheads. That is, he said that unless the United States could continue airburst tests over dummy missile silo fields and control centers, there would be no way of telling how the electrical and communications cable networks connecting these to one another would respond to the huge electromagnetic fields, ion flux and gamma radiation which would result from an enemy attack. Several of us expressed disbelief that physicists were so completely unable to estimate the effects. When he persisted I suggested that it ought to be possible to use ridiculously large amounts of lead, iron and copper shielding on the cables at a fraction of the cost of the installations, and possibly at a monetary cost not much greater than that of the tests, to eliminate these effects. He fell back, apparently startled, and then renewed his argument. Some of us left the meeting convinced that the possible loss of his toys was bothering him much more than the threat to what he called the "proof-testing" program. Interestingly enough, this briefing was classified secret yet Senator Barry Goldwater several weeks later gave exactly the same arguments to the press. But this did not free us of restraint and we had the distinct feeling, not for the first time, that the security system was being used politically.

Not all of RAND's military work was to such ends. On an earlier brief visit to RAND I spent time with two men who went on to become subcabinet officials in Defense and in the Bureau of the Budget during the Kennedy-Johnson period. One of them has since returned to RAND in a senior capacity. These two men told me that almost accidentally they had learned a year or more before of the air force's plans for a 24-hour airborne alert strategic bombing force. The plan called for a flight of B-52s, loaded with thermonuclear warheads, to be aloft at all times. Each flight would head toward the North Pole from a United States base, to reach a certain point in the Arctic region by a specified time. If by then they had not received a coded radio signal calling them back, they were to cut off radio contact, open their sealed bombing orders and proceed to bomb their designated targets. The two staff men described their horror at learning this. By pointing out that not only was the reliability of this plan dangerously dependent on satisfactory radio reception in an area (near a magnetic pole) of great radio interference, but that it placed far too great a burden of power in the hands of one man, the flight commander, they succeeded (although with difficulty) in getting the air force to convert this plan into the well-known "fail-safe" one in which planes were to proceed only if ordered by coded radio signal to do so. The possibility of accidental thermonuclear war has no doubt been reduced as a result of their success.

Herman Kahn was at RAND for many years. More than

any other single person, he should probably be given major credit for persuading senior military people in the late fifties and early sixties that they should not think casually of "nuking" as the first response to any radar anomaly in a time of international tension. For his pains, and because he was heavily in favor of a large fallout shelter program (which the air force objected to because of not being able to claim jurisdiction over it), Kahn was apparently given the polite bum's rush from RAND in 1961.

Most of RAND's work was based on a premise which can best be described as a perverse compound of positivism and arrogance. A careful positivist might say that in principle, most human processes might be shown to operate according to a number of fundamental regularities or laws; very few of those laws could now be described and almost no computations could confidently be conducted on their basis now or in the foreseeable future. But RAND and a few other groups tended to operate as if these laws were sufficiently in our grasp for significant decisions, involving vast amounts of human and material resources to be made on the basis of that knowledge.

How was this assumption of such a reliable basis for action made in the first place, and how was it used?

RAND was the first major organization wholly formed by an intellectual movement using systems analysis—the application of probability theory and logic and a sense of urgency to the study of systems of moderate complexity and of a middle range of articulatedness. Thus, systems analysis of the progress of a submarine through a known body of water, of the pursuit of one aircraft with known flight characteristics, of the impact on a particular landscape or seascape of the detonation at a specified altitude of a particular size and type of nuclear weapon, of the flow through a network, the pileup and/or depletion of material at various points in the network when the layout and capacity of the components of the network are known, were typical of problems handled in the early days by systems analysts at RAND and elsewhere. Characteristically, these analysts were not specialists in aircraft or naval tactics, bombing analysis or traffic management. They tended to think of themselves as generalists, that is, as experts in the use of analytical techniques. As generalists they accepted objectives or goals (or what are known in larger contexts as values) from their employers or clients, and worked out techniques for maximal approach to them with minimum expenditures of effort or resources.

So long as the limitations of this sort of generalist analysis were understood—when the importance of errors arising from unfamiliarity with empirical detail was minimized by the relatively tight articulation of the system, and when the cost of error was confined by the relatively confined character of the problem—then systems analysis was useful and safe both for military and nonmilitary systems. However, the normal arrogance of the technician who has had successes where others have had failures led to the assertion of competence in much larger, less confined, less well-articulated processes. The result has been a greater admixture of failures with successes. And the failures have been more spectacular and costly. Moreover, they have been met all too frequently by the "well, back to the drawing board" attitude of the technician, which, in really catastrophic situations, is an acceptance of no responsibility at all.

This transfer of abstract analysis to real cosmic threat situations (such as the Cuban missile crisis) is characteristic of the RAND systems-analysis approach to human problems. Similar such extensions of generalist competence can be found in and out of RAND. Daniel Ellsberg had spent a few years at RAND doing studies of deterrence and war-threat crises in a world of nuclear powers before he began occasionally briefing people on the White House War Room staff and in the Office of the Secretary of Defense on the subject of crisis management.

A specialist expert in high-altitude photography— Amron Katz—became a generalist expert in the politics of disarmament. A specialist expert in the testing of high-yield nuclear weapons—Herman Kahn—became a generalist expert in the politics of escalation and in almost any other subject in which he was interested. Specialist experts in cost analysis—the group that moved with Charles Hitch from RAND into the Office of the Comptroller and the Office of Systems Analysis in the Office of the Secretary of Defense under Robert McNamara— became generalist experts and enunciated design principles for a supersonic fighter-bomber for the air force and the navy, counter to the strong opinion of experienced procurement and flight officers in both services. Using program budgeting and cost-effectiveness analysis, they planned the entire force structure of the United States defense system.

This sort of thinking—generalizing, often successfully, on the basis of intellectual skill in handling limited, simple problems to the treatment of more complex, less confined, more bloody problems, while at the same time not really accepting responsibility; seeing human problems as games which can be replayed, again without acceptance of responsibility—came out of RAND and a few other places (such as the Institute for Defense Analyses, Harvard and MIT) and lodged in the White House, the Pentagon and the State Department in the persons of McNamara and his whiz kids, the Bundy brothers, W. W. Rostow and others. Vietnam, the Dominican adventure, the missile crisis and F-111 should all be understood as the fruits of that sort of thinking.

Within RAND there has always been a kind of recognized order of brilliance, and admiration for it as a quality. Those who were especially opposed to the war in Vietnam and who were therefore most frequently subject to criticisms that they were being unpatriotic or were confused were not regarded within the organization as brilliant. The question that naturally comes to mind, now that it is generally agreed that something has been rotten in Vietnam all along, is this: What is brilliance and what value is it if it is associated with dimness in recognizing such a state of affairs, especially with so much more information available than the general public has?

Brilliance, of course, must be understood as a flashy, narrow, technical facility. The keen mind that can weave its way through complex technical issues is considered brilliant. But wisdom is yet another quality, different from brilliance. Wisdom involves making ethical judgments and reasoning from ethical positions, while brilliance does not. RAND has had lots of brilliance and very little wisdom.

After all this, it is reasonable to ask why I was at RAND. All told, I worked in RAND-like situations for five years, although the two years before I came to RAND and the one year after I left were spent at places that only vaguely resembled it. They did work for the Department of Defense but almost exclusively in logistics. Still, clearances were required. I regarded that five-year episode as a potentially interesting experience, a sort of trial by ordeal, and went into it at a time when I was ready to leave the academic situation in which I then found myself. When I was invited to join RAND in 1963 I set only one condition: that I not be pressed to do war-connected work. This condition was accepted, but shortly after I arrived the promise began to be eroded. I resisted and during the two years I was there my superiors and I fought constantly. I'm sure that RAND did not get its money's worth from me because I kept insisting on the original bargain. Finally, in the midst of a financial debacle and a sizeable reduction in personnel, I was fired. I felt relieved. I had joined RAND believing I could stay uninvolved with those things which I vaguely knew were going on there. I stayed because I was fascinated and horrified, as was probably the case with others. Still others have stayed because they felt that they might make some difference and yet others because RAND was one of the few places in which they can do their own non-war-related work. Most, of course, have stayed because a RAND job is, by most indices, a good job and because the work is not sufficiently disturbing to cause them to leave.

What is apparent to me now—and it is at the heart of the tragedy of the Ellsbergs and all the other whiz kids and men who ever went to Washington from RAND or anywhere else—is that defense think tanks engender habits of thought which are amoral because they appear to separate analysis and responsibility. When minds that are morally relaxed grapple with problems that are loaded with moral freight, they are likely to come up with immoral policies. Only the burden of responsibility can be depended on to make people face the implications of their work. It is easier for the bomber pilot to unleash death on thousands of civilians than for the rifleman to do the same to dozens.

Moreover, RAND has not simply generated such solutions within its own walls and by means of its alumni in Washington. It has been emulated in a wide variety of ways. There are, first of all, a number of other defense think tanks which were and are patterned after RAND, but because it was the first and the most successful it is still the most influential. Secondly, whenever a proposal is made for an institute to be set up which will use highly trained technical skill to deal in a detached abstract way with any of a wide range of nonmilitary problems or tasks of society, the image of RAND is invoked as a reference image, frequently as a goal. Thirdly, RAND was for many years and may still be a large influence on university campuses. It has spent significant sums of money for work done on those campuses and, even more important, it brings many university faculty members and dozens of graduate students to its quarters for extended stays each year. RAND money buys their time and services and may well affect them, although probably less intensively, in ways which are similar to the ways in which I have suggested it affects its own full-time people. Hence RAND and the other defense think tanks may be a source of moral infection which ought to be taken seriously.

Ought we to continue to operate research institutes and research-funding institutes which purport to conduct or support value-neutral analyses of important value-laden policy questions? Should we continue to place brilliant minds in positions where they can influence or bring about important decisions without responsibly facing their implications and without the restraint of fundamental moral commitments? The price has been very high and not all the bills are in yet.

April 1972

FURTHER READING SUGGESTED BY THE AUTHOR:

The RAND Corporation: A Case Study of a Nonprofit Advisory Corporation by B. L. R. Smith (Cambridge: Harvard University Press, 1966).

Systems Analysis and Policy Planning by E. S. Quade (New York: American Elsevier, 1968).

Studies of War, Nuclear and Conventional by P. M. S. Blackett (New York: Hill and Wang, 1962).

Jessie Bernard ("Report from Iron Mountain") was professor of sociology at Pennsylvania State University. She is the author of *Academic Women, Marriage and Family Among Negroes* and *The Sex Game.*

Kenneth E. Boulding ("The Deadly Industry: War and the International System," "Comments on Report from Iron Mountain") is professor of economics at the University of Colorado. For further information, see the back cover.

Leonard Duhl ("Report from Iron Mountain") is a psychiatrist serving as special assistant to the Secretary of the Department of Housing and Urban Development.

Irving Louis Horowitz ("The Pentagon Papers and Social Science") is distinguished professor of sociology at Rutgers University. He is editor-in-chief of *Society* magazine and director of *Studies in Comparative International Development.* Among his recent books are *Foundations of Political Sociology, Three Worlds of Development* (2nd edition), and *Cuban Communism* (2nd edition) published by Transaction Books.

Marvin Kalkstein ("ABM and the Arms Race") is a faculty member of the Experimental College at the State University of New York at Stony Brook. His recent work includes "Time for a Fresh Look at U.S. Nuclear Weapons Test Policy" and an article in *Science and the Future of Man,* edited by Bentley Glass.

Louis Kriesberg ("Non-governmental Organizations") is professor of sociology at Syracuse University and a research associate at the Youth Development Center. His research has focused on poverty, fatherless families and public housing, and he has edited *Social Processes in International Relations: A Reader.*

Raoul Naroll ("Does Military Deterrence Deter?") is professor of anthropology at State University of New York at Buffalo. He is the author of *Preliminary Index of Social Development* and *Data Quality Control.*

Marc Pilisuk ("Comments on Report from Iron Mountain") is professor in residence at the School of Social Welfare at the University of California, Berkeley. With Phyllis Pilisuk he is editor of *Poor Americans: How the White Poor Live* and the forthcoming *How We Lost the War on Poverty,* both published by Transaction Books.

Elwin H. Powell ("Paradoxes of the Warfare State") is associate professor of sociology at the State University of New York at Buffalo. He has written on the evolution of the American city, suicide and the beat generation. He has also studied the sociology of war.

Anatole Rapoport ("Comments on Report from Iron Mountain") is professor of mental health at the Mental Health Research Center of the University of Michigan. His main areas of interest are mathematical theories of nervous systems of learning and communication, the philosophy of science, and mathematical model of behavior.

John R. Raser ("The Failure of Fail-Safe") is associate professor of political studies at the University of Otago, Dunedin, New Zealand.

Milton J. Rosenberg ("New Ways to Reduce Distrust Between the United States and Russia") is professor of social psychology at the University of Chicago. Senior author of *Attitude Organization and Change* and co-author of *Theories of Cognitive Consistency*, he completed a book for Transaction, *Beyond Conflict and Containment: Critical Studies of Military and Foreign Policy.*

Henry S. Rowen ("Report from Iron Mountain") is president of the RAND Corporation.

Bruce M. Russett ("The Price of War") is professor of political science at Yale University and editor of the *Journal of Conflict Resolution.* His recent books include *What Price Vigilance: The Burdens of National Defense; No Clear and Present Danger: A Skeptical View of the United States Entry into World War II;* and *Military Force and American Society* (co-editor).

Murray Weidenbaum ("Report from Iron Mountain") is Edward Mallinckrodt Distinguished Professor at Washington University, St. Louis. He is a member of President Nixon's Rent Advisory Board. His publications include *The Modern Public Sector* and numerous journal articles.

Robert J. Wolfson ("In the Hawk's Nest: An Inside Story of the Workings of the RAND Corporation") is professor of economics at Syracuse University and research fellow at the Educational Policy Research Center. Formerly associated with the journal of *Economic Development and Social Change,* he spent several years at think tanks in the Santa Monica area, including the RAND Corporation.